PRAISE FOR *DEPRESSION, ANXIETY, AND OTHER THINGS WE DON'T WANT TO TALK ABOUT*

"I work with Christian leaders from all over the country and have seen firsthand how desperately we need to be talking about depression and anxiety. What prior generations considered taboo, the leaders of today and tomorrow consider essential. If the church is going to be the hands and feet of Christ, we have to ensure we're caring for the minds of those who serve. Whether you're new to the conversation of mental health or intimately familiar with its complexities, Waller's book has something for you. As long as I've known Ryan it's been pretty clear that this topic and this book has been his life mission. I can't wait for you to read this. A must-read."

—Grant Skeldon, author of *The Passion Generation*
and Next Gen Director at Q

"Having personally suffered from a very public mental breakdown, this book speaks directly to my heart. Christians are often hesitant to say, 'I'm not okay,' but this book speaks directly to the courage we must have to bring our collective anxiety, depression, and mental health to the light. God made us all imperfect, but what will we do with it all? Here, Waller shares his very personal journey, and shows that it *is* possible to heal—if we face our truths. Our very lives depend on it."

—Jason Russell, filmmaker and activist

"'You are not alone.' Ryan hits the nail on the head. As someone who struggles with major depressive episodes, I found Ryan's book both enlightening and practical in how I can better manage my depression with the help of my compassionate community."

—Brian Cuban, author of *The Addicted Lawyer*

"This book is a wonderful and sensitive encouragement for anyone whose life has become unbearably dark and for those who seek to help them. This book vulnerably and compassionately addresses the conversations we have run from for far too long. This book offers a reliable resource to understanding mental illness from a biblical perspective. Ryan Casey Waller has a way of spreading grace and hope while bearing the burdens of the afflicted."

—Rashawn Copeland, author and founder of I'm So Blessed Daily

"*Depression, Anxiety, and Other Things We Don't Want to Talk About* is a compassionate playbook for people struggling with their mental health, and for friends and family members searching for effective ways to give support. Through scripture, science, and practical tips—paired with Waller's own powerful story—we are compelled to think beyond our perceptions and act beyond our comfort zones to create new opportunities for healing."

—Shelby Abeyta, campaign director of Okay to Say

"Thank God someone has expanded the conversation on mental health and faith. Ryan Casey Waller, in *Depression, Anxiety, and Other Things We Don't Want to Talk About*, has exposed some very important pain points in our field and opened them up for further discussion with our patients, colleagues, and the public. He is not only an excellent therapist to whom I regularly refer my patients, but a consummate thinker and organizer of thoughts. We all need this book to help mental health move forward."

—Lee Spencer MD, board certified addiction psychiatrist

"I've been convinced for a long time that churches tend to be the scariest places, rather than the safest places, for fallen and broken people. That is sad and maddening to me and my hope is that this exceptional book will be used by God to help turn that tide. What I love about this book is its sober realism—its willingness to acknowledge that we are all broken people, living in a broken world with other broken people. There is no spiritualized fluff here. And because of its raw honesty in describing things as they are, rather than as we would like them to be, there is hope. Thank you, Ryan, for reminding us that it's okay to not be okay."

—Tullian Tchividjian, pastor of The Sanctuary in Jupiter, Florida, and author of *Jesus + Nothing = Everything*

"The first author since Brené Brown to touch me so deeply and teach me so profoundly. In this book Waller reminds us that mental health is fluid, lifelong, and often very messy. Fortunately, Waller tells us we have a God who inhabits our illness and will not abandon us to it. To know this truth, however, we must talk about it. And talk about it Waller does. With wit and sincerity, Waller is honest about the fact that mental illness does not discriminate, meaning it can happen to anyone at any given time. No one is immune. Consequently, Waller encourages us to delve into understanding mental illness before we find ourselves plunging into its abyss. In this heartfelt book that combines psychology and the Christian faith in a way I've never before seen, Waller offers a way forward that is not only full of hope but also chock-full of practical take-aways from one who has not only studied this subject but also lived it."

—Susan Hawk, fellow co-sufferer, youngest elected district court judge in Texas, and first female district attorney in Dallas county history

ALSO BY RYAN CASEY WALLER

Broken

DEPRESSION, ANXIETY, AND OTHER THINGS WE DON'T WANT TO TALK ABOUT

RYAN CASEY WALLER

NELSON
BOOKS

An Imprint of Thomas Nelson

Published in Nashville, Tennessee, by Nelson Books, an imprint of Thomas Nelson. Nelson Books and Thomas Nelson are registered trademarks of HarperCollins Christian Publishing, Inc.

Thomas Nelson titles may be purchased in bulk for educational, business, fundraising, or sales promotional use. For information, please email SpecialMarkets@ThomasNelson.com.

Library of Congress Cataloging-in-Publication Data

Names: Waller, Ryan Casey, author.
Title: Depression, anxiety, and other things we don't want to talk about / Ryan Casey Waller.
Description: Nashville, Tennessee : Nelson Books, [2020] | Includes bibliographical references. | Summary: "A pastor and licensed psychotherapist himself suffering from depression and anxiety takes on the relationship of mental health and faith while addressing the role of self-care, compassion, and restoration"-- Provided by publisher.
Identifiers: LCCN 2020028545 (print) | LCCN 2020028546 (ebook) | ISBN 9781400221325 (paperback) | ISBN 9781400221332 (epub)
Subjects: LCSH: Mental health--Religious aspects--Christianity. | Christianity--Psychology. | Psychology, Religious.
Classification: LCC BT732.4 .W35 2020 (print) | LCC BT732.4 (ebook) | DDC 261.8/322--dc23
LC record available at https://lccn.loc.gov/2020028545
LC ebook record available at https://lccn.loc.gov/2020028546

Printed in the United States of America

21 22 23 24 25   LSC   10 9 8 7 6 5 4 3 2 1

To Caroline, Ford, and Charles.
Everything I do is because of you.
Except for my mistakes.
Those are on me.

CONTENTS

AUTHOR NOTE   XI

INTRODUCTION   XIII

ONE: YOU'RE NOT ALONE   1
TWO: WHAT IS MENTAL HEALTH?   17
THREE: WHAT IS MENTAL ILLNESS?   29
FOUR: WHY DOES GOD ALLOW MENTAL ILLNESS?   47
FIVE: THIS IS NOT A DRILL   61
SIX: ABUNDANT LIFE FOR ALL   69
SEVEN: EPIDEMIC   79
EIGHT: THE PROBLEM OF SUICIDE   91
NINE: WHO ARE WE?   109
TEN: TALK THERAPY   127
ELEVEN: MEDICATION   147
TWELVE: PEOPLE   161
THIRTEEN: PUTTING TREATMENT ALL TOGETHER   175

CONCLUSION   187

CONTENTS

A FINAL THOUGHT FOR CHRISTIANS
WHO DON'T SUFFER FROM MENTAL ILLNESS 191

MENTAL ILLNESS: A MOST BRIEF HISTORY 195

A PRIMER ON DEPRESSION AND ANXIETY 203

COMMON SIGNS OF SUICIDAL THOUGHTS AND BEHAVIORS 217

SUGGESTED READING 221

ACKNOWLEDGMENTS 223

NOTES 225

ABOUT THE AUTHOR 235

AUTHOR NOTE

While the author is a mental health professional, the information in this book is not prescriptive to any individual experience. If you are currently depressed or in crisis, please seek a mental health provider who can address your individual issues. If you believe you are in immediate danger, dial 911.

While the narratives in this book represent true experiences, names and other identifying facts have been altered to provide anonymity.

INTRODUCTION

You bought a book about things we don't want to talk about. That's impressive. I'm proud of you. I'm also grateful for you because you just put some coin in my pocket. For real, it's much appreciated. I guess I'll keep buying that daily $2.33 cup of Starbucks coffee my wife would prefer I brew at home.

But seriously, you chose this book, and now I'm wondering why. It's not like there's *not* an episode of something extremely awesome streaming on Netflix or Disney+. I mean, are we living in the Golden Age of Television or what? Anyhoo, you're not watching TV. Instead, you've chosen to focus your attention on my book, and that's really got me curious about what's going on inside of you and all around you.

Maybe you're feeling sad about a life stressor like a divorce or a job loss, and you want to know if your low mood is "normal" or dipping into the realm of clinical depression. A lot of people wonder about this.

Maybe when you wake up in the morning your mind fills with dread at the prospect of facing the day, and you're curious if it's just because you don't like your job or because something more serious is happening with you psychologically.

Maybe in recent months you've noticed that you're drinking more alcohol than you have in the past. Now you're considering cutting back and wondering how to best go about it. Or maybe you've already tried cutting back but haven't been as successful as you'd hoped to be, and now you can't stop taking those online quizzes that promise to tell you whether you're an alcoholic (been there). You're wondering: Are these tests accurate? And if they are, does that mean you need to start attending a twelve-step group where you drink stale coffee and bare your soul to strangers and collect anniversary chips? Does that also mean you have to be abstinent from alcohol for the rest of your life? A lot of questions are coming up at once.

Maybe your spouse or child is battling a mental health issue, and you feel overwhelmed or bewildered by what your loved one is experiencing. You want to help, you want to understand, but you're just not certain what to do or where to turn for trustworthy information.

Or maybe you're one of the many, many Christians who suffer in the mind or body but have felt too ashamed to speak up about it. You know you need help, but admitting this is hard because it feels like you're letting down God or admitting that your faith in him isn't strong enough. I know a lot of Christians who feel this way. I used to be one of them.

I don't know what, exactly, you're going through. All I know is that I'm really glad you picked this book up because mental health and mental illness are, in some ways, the final spiritual and medical frontier. There is so much we don't know. We need to be honest about that. But there is also a lot we do know, and it's absolutely critical we spread that information far and wide.

So, if you've come here for healing, I pray you'll find it. If you've come here to help someone who is hurting, I wish you well on the journey. And if you've come here to simply learn more in an effort to stand alongside those who suffer, I applaud you for your efforts.

Speaking of effort, let's get to work.

The sun rises and with it the reality of what happened the night before. Your brain is bathed in cortisol, bringing forth an unrivaled onslaught of unmitigated dread. Your memories taunt you, forcing you to relive the sequence of events. It's foggy, but from beneath the sheets of your bed you're able to piece together the events from the prior evening.

You have finished delivering your boozy sermon and are walking on unsteady legs back to the altar to lead the congregation in the recitation of the Nicene Creed when, out of nowhere, another pastor appears to take your place. He whispers something in your ear. Moments later you are being interrogated in a back room, out of sight from the congregation, by your friends—people who love and care for you. Folks you love in return. They want to know if you're sick. They're worried that maybe you're having a stroke. Your speech was slurred during the sermon. At one point you almost fell over and had to grab hold of the podium to remain upright. They ask you what's happening. Should they call a doctor?

God bless these saints; they give you every benefit of the doubt.

There are three of them standing in close quarters. The one who knows you best asks the question that has surely crossed everyone's mind, but up until this moment, no one has wanted to voice it.

"Have you been drinking?"

There is a pause. The pause tells everyone everything they need to know. You are guilty of this offense. You have been drinking more than you should in recent months. Your wife has confronted you about it. She wants you to cut back, perhaps drop the habit altogether. She's suggested you reach out to a particular friend who has been sober for a decade or so, but you're not ready for that.

Whenever you encounter a self-described alcoholic you silently wonder whether you are one too. You have closely studied the DSM-5 to determine if you meet the criteria for substance use disorder. There are options for mild, moderate, or severe. It all depends on how honest you want to be. On certain days the answer is rather clear to you. It's the uncertain days, however, where you've chosen to couch your reality. At least for now.

"Have you been drinking?"

They must smell it on your breath. The questions about sickness and a stroke are their noble attempts at allowing you to keep your dignity. They don't want to accuse you of anything. You are their leader. They're desperately hoping you will lead righteously in this moment and police yourself.

Still.

You make like Peter and deny it. You become even more defensive. You raise your voice as the congregation in the church continues to confess the ancient words of faith.

We believe in the Holy Spirit, the Lord, the giver of life,
who proceeds from the Father and the Son.
With the Father and the Son he is worshiped and glorified.

He has spoken through the Prophets.
We believe in one holy catholic and apostolic Church.
We acknowledge one baptism for the forgiveness of sins.
We look for the resurrection of the dead,
and the life of the world to come. Amen.[1]

They then begin the Prayers of the People, prayers you should be leading them in. It never crosses your mind that they might be able to hear their pastor accusing his friends of creating something out of nothing. Deep down you know these friends only want what is best for you. Not a single one is looking at you with malice. Only with love. And confusion.

There is a gentle offer to drive you home, but you refuse because you believe you can still bully your way back into the church to do your job. You can definitely finish the service, you say. This is a major overreaction. This moment can be overcome and forgotten. It will be nothing but a blip on the radar. This is all a ridiculous misunderstanding.

Thank God your friends will not be moved. They have already discussed the matter. A decision has been made. You're no longer in charge. The authority has been ceded. You have come to church drunk, and the people of God are not going to allow you to desecrate this worship service any more than you already have.

You end the conversation and storm out of the church. One dear brother follows, pleading with you to let him take you home. Instead, you choose to drive home drunk at the very moment you should be sipping sacred wine and eating blessed and broken bread.

YOU'RE NOT ALONE

The circumstances that bring mental illness to light are often a surprise—to all people involved. Sometimes it's a friend or loved one, or perhaps someone you respected and admired from afar, who you never imagined to be struggling until something happened. Sometimes, as it was in my case, it's you.

After that disaster of a Sunday, I couldn't deny it. My life suddenly felt like the chapter ending in *Gone Girl* when you realize Amy's been lying to you the whole time. When I revisited what had happened after a full night's rest, my sober brain did the most righteous double take.

There is no way I went to church drunk.

That did not just happen.

That could not *have just happened.*

But, oh, my dear brothers and sisters, it most certainly did happen.

The wildest part, however, was that if you would have asked me how I was doing on the afternoon before I went back for that evening service, I'd have told you I was fine. And I would have believed it. *Nothing wrong here, thank you very much. Just another guy doing what needs to be done to make it through a Sunday. Taking care of my family and serving the kingdom. Sometimes that service requires afternoon booze and an Ambien to help with the power nap. What could possibly be wrong with that?*

In reality I was spiritually dead, burned out, depressed, and drinking *way* too much. But I had a job to do, so I didn't have time to be honest about all of that. I kid you not; I had no clue my world was about to blow up.

Which is mostly how mental illness works. You don't know you have it until it's all up in your grill trying to destroy your life. This happens, most often, because getting honest with ourselves about what's going on in our hearts and minds is a difficult thing to do. So mental illness frequently goes undiagnosed until, well, it just can't anymore because really weird things start happening.

You break down crying on the kitchen floor at the thought of making a peanut butter and jelly sandwich for your kid. Didn't that used to be an easy thing to do? The alarm clock signals a brand-new day has begun. A wave of anxiety washes over you. Didn't the rising sun used to excite you? You check your work email to see what needs to be accomplished. Instead of getting to work you sit frozen, staring at the to-do list as if it were a torture device sent to assault your brain and deprive you of any semblance of competence or peace. A friend criticizes a decision you made, and suddenly the inner critic that used to only occasionally condemn you now speaks up 24-7, reminding you that you're worthless and stupid. When these experiences bombard our lives, we either bury them with drugs and alcohol or get honest about the fact that something is awry.

But until then, most of us pretend we aren't depressed, which is a fabulous way to make sure we're still depressed tomorrow. Others of us overspiritualize the situation, which is also not helpful. Praying your chronic anxiety goes away (something I do without shame) is not—in and of itself—a sufficient strategy for healing. Especially if we can't admit that we struggle with anxiety and depression in the first place.

I understand this is tough sledding. Addressing our mental health is more complicated than addressing other aspects of our health, especially for Christians. I personally put off seeing a therapist for ten years before I finally broke down and admitted I needed psychiatric help. I was convinced I could rid myself of anxiety if I prayed hard enough, read my Bible long enough, and served other people sincerely enough. But there's a secret I've discovered that gives us the power we need to enter this conversation with the honesty required for it to be helpful.

Do you want to know what it is?

You.

Me.

All of us.

Are in this together.

And together we can see this thing through.

I am not speaking as Moses from the mountaintop but rather as an Israelite from the valley below. I may be a mental health professional with expertise to offer, but I am first and foremost a cosufferer who knows how painful and difficult battles with mental illness can be.

If you picked up this book because you're currently suffering from any kind of mental anguish, please know that, even though it might genuinely feel like it, you aren't alone. You also might feel like no one has ever felt as bad as you do in this moment. Please believe me when I say these are some of depression's favorite lies to tell—lies that, if believed, will do nothing but make your path to healing more difficult to traverse.

Just a few weeks ago I was feeling really depressed. It was the third Monday of the month, which is the day I attend a terrific support group for lawyers who suffer from depression. (Yes, I used to be a lawyer. Maybe that's my problem?) But because depression is really good at its job, I almost didn't go to the meeting. All I wanted to do was lie down in bed and pretend that *not* fighting back would help me feel better. See how smart depression is? If you let it, it'll convince you to do the exact opposite of what's best for you. Sort of like the internet.

I said to Caroline, my wife: "I don't think I'm going to the meeting tonight."

"Why not?" she asked.

"I don't feel like it."

"Okay," she said, "why don't we have dinner and maybe you can go a little late?"

"Okay," I said, feeling immediate relief at the prospect of *not* feeling better that evening.

I'm telling you, depression is wicked smart.

So we ate our dinner. When we finished, Caroline said, "How are you feeling now? Gonna go?"

"Nah," I replied. "I want to stay home with you and the boys."

"You've been home a lot lately. Don't *not* go because of us. We're fine. Really."

I knew she was right. When I was a pastor (I used to be one of those too. Maybe *that's* my problem?) I missed a lot of dinners at home. Now that I'm a writer and therapist I'm almost always home in the evenings. Depression might be smart, but my wife is smarter. Caroline knew I didn't have any reason for not going other than not wanting to go, which actually isn't a reason at all but depression masquerading as an excuse.

"Yeah," I said, "but I *am* going to be gone tomorrow evening for that banquet thing with Terry, so I had better just stay home tonight."

"You do whatever is best for you, but tonight's an easy night." She glanced over at our two boys, Ford and Charles (ages six and four), who were finishing up their dinners. "Charles already had his bath, and Ford will shower on his own. So, it's easy breezy—"

"Lemon squeezy!" Ford said, finishing her sentence.

Charles laughed at his older brother, and I gave in because children are magic like that.

When I got to the parking lot of the hotel where the meeting was being held, I stayed in my car for about fifteen minutes. At this point I was really late. To make matters worse, my good friend was scheduled to be the speaker that evening, and I knew he had saved a seat for me at the table in the front of the room. Still, I just sat there feeling awful.

I should mention that when I'm feeling well, I'm obnoxiously punctual because I believe respecting other people's time is tremendously important. I despise being late. But depression isn't only smart, it's enormously powerful. It can take your deeply held values and throw them out the window, making you do things you'd never do otherwise. It can also prevent you from doing the very things you adore.

Finally, I pulled out my phone in an effort to externalize my feelings. There is mounting evidence that simply writing down how we feel, uninterrupted, for a few minutes a day is wildly curative for depression. I decided to give it a shot. This is what I punched into my phone:

Depression takes so many forms.

Here's how it looked for me today:

All day I felt like a failure. An unending loop played in my head telling me that I have failed everyone in my life who loves me. My thoughts primarily focused on my wife and children who deserve a father who isn't a failure. They deserve a father who is loving, financially successful, upbeat, and well liked by others. But what they have instead is me. A person who is none of these things. I am a failure. This is what my depression tells me, and this is how I feel. Facts and reality mean nothing. I know (I think) that none of this is actually true, and yet knowing this does absolutely nothing to make me feel differently. The only truth that matters is the one that lives inside my head.

My feelings of failure also made it damn near impossible to think clearly today. I struggled mightily to write only a few words. Words that probably suck and will be of no use to anyone.

On top of all of this is a pervasive boredom that has replaced my interest in topics I know I like. I went for a jog today (a near miracle) and listened to a book on my phone that has mesmerized me for weeks. But today I had to force myself to keep listening. I know, intellectually, that I am interested in what the writer is saying. I can also appreciate the fact that the book is well written. I also know that I want to know what will happen next in the story. And yet, today, I do not care and feel as though I will never care about it or anything else I used to care about ever again.

This is depression.

And it is hard.

On that happy note, I put my phone away, got out of my car, and walked into the meeting, convinced the next hour would be nothing more than a white-knuckled ride through my own embattled mind. The only good news was that, since I was already egregiously late, the meeting would necessarily end sooner as opposed to later. Just for good measure, however, I ducked into the men's room on my way inside. Eventually, I entered the meeting room, head down, found my way to my reserved seat up front, and sat down.

Nothing extraordinary happened in the meeting. A few people shared their stories. My buddy, who is a clinical psychologist, gave his talk and it was great. Another friend, who was very recently suicidal and subsequently hospitalized, gave me a big hug, appearing genuinely happy to be alive. In this group that's no small thing. So that was *really* great to see.

When the meeting was over, I headed home. I wasn't suddenly cured or anything, but I'd be lying if I said I didn't feel *much* better than I did before the meeting. The dread of the day had almost miraculously passed from me. As I walked back to my car, I felt light and excited to go home and kiss my wife and hug my children, who would by now be snuggled up tightly in their beds. The thought of watching a TV show crossed my mind, and I felt a pang of interest, which felt hella good. Maybe life would be fun again.

Maybe.

What changed? How did I arrive at the meeting in such bad shape only to emerge, less than an hour later, feeling hopeful and energized?

It's simple, really. In the meeting I was reminded of what is perhaps the most important truth to hold on to during any struggle with mental health.

I'm not alone.

You're not alone.

Understanding and believing this is the first step on the journey toward mental health.

DIFFERENT SHAPES AND SIZES

There are so many of us who battle our mental health. And it's not because we are failures or worthless or bad as our brains so often try and convince us that we are. It's simply that we suffer in our minds as a result of a chemical imbalance in the brain, or a trauma experienced in childhood, or any number of other psychological and environmental factors.

Some of us battle mental illness like others of us battle our cholesterol. It's nothing to be ashamed of. Rather, it's a fact of life to be taken very seriously. Plain and simple. What's not simple about mental illness, however, is that, like most complicated human phenomena, it goes by many names and is known in many ways. Which is just another way of saying mental illness rarely means the same thing to two different people.

Some struggle to get out of bed in the morning. Others stay away from their beds for days on end, avoiding sleep like the plague when in a manic state. Some overeat, while others have no appetite at all. Some of us call these conditions depression, while others are more familiar with names like anxiety or mania. Some know it by the way it affects their relationship to food, and they call it bulimia or anorexia nervosa. For others it comes by way of alcohol or a doctor's prescription, and they call it a substance use disorder.

The suffering shape-shifts and manifests itself in our lives in so many ways the professionals who categorize it can barely keep pace.

The current *Diagnostic and Statistical Manual of Mental Disorders*, the manual that guides mental health professionals in making diagnoses, is now in its fifth incarnation since its first publication in 1952. The newest edition contains 265 different diagnoses.

The first edition had roughly two dozen.

And consider this: the 265 diagnoses do not discriminate. They do not care what kind of job you have or whether you have a job at all. They pay no mind to the last name of your family or the prestige of your alma mater. They fear no amount of talent, money, or plastic surgery. Nor do they pass out exemption cards for active religious affiliation, ethnic background, or hours spent volunteering in your community. Mental illness can and does affect every kind of person on earth.

This is daunting, for sure. But there is another way to look at this reality that I, as one who suffers, find encouraging. The *DSM* didn't explode in size because psychiatrists were bored and had nothing else to do. It grew because people were suffering, and these doctors and other mental health professionals took their pain seriously enough to study it and try to provide a common language for all of us to speak about it. That tells me at least two things. First, smart people have been working on these issues. I like when intelligent people work on issues I care about. Second, it's another data point to contradict the lie my brain loves to tell about me being the only one who struggles. If I were, the *DSM* wouldn't be hundreds of pages long. Instead, it'd have one single page with my ugly mug plastered on it. Thank God this is the case, because my not being alone means you're not alone either. Can I get an amen?

We need to shout this from the mountaintops, because if we don't, mental illness will scream at us during the day and whisper to us at night that no other person on the planet is as worthless as we are and that no other person has ever felt as much pain as we're currently feeling. The voice will be powerful and convincing, but the voice will also be untrue. Repeat this with me: we're not alone, never have been, nor will we ever be.

CHOOSE TO BELIEVE

Jamie Tworkowski is the founder of To Write Love on Her Arms (TWLOHA), an organization that works to destigmatize mental illness and connect those who suffer with the help they need. In his book, *If You Feel Too Much*, he wrote:

> You're not alone in this. If yesterday was a hard day, you weren't the only one who felt that way. Maybe there are things you need to say. Maybe there's a letter you need to write, an e-mail to send. Maybe it's going to take a long time and today you just need to call a friend and begin to be honest. Maybe things are really heavy or it's just too painful. . . . Maybe it's time to find some help. Help is real. Hope is real. These things are possible. You're not alone.
>
> The thing about the idea that you're not alone is that it doesn't do us much good if it's just an idea. We have to do something with it. It's like having no money and then someone hands you a check. You have to take it to the bank. You have to do something with it. Maybe hope is like that. Maybe community is like that. Maybe relationships are like that. We have to choose these things. We have to say they're real and possible and important. We have to say some things out loud. We have to choose to believe that our story matters, along with the stories of the people we love.[1]

We have to *choose* to believe. I absolutely love that. Especially in light of the fact that there was only one thing God said *wasn't* good when he created this world of ours: that man was alone.

That's it. The sky was good. The sea was good. God even declared that the filthy little critters creeping along the earth were good. But not us humans. Nope. For us to be good we needed something else. And not just anything else, we needed *someone* else. Human beings do better when connected to one another.

In 1760 a Spanish bishop wrote to his superiors in Rome, letting them know that some of the children living in foundling homes were dying despite the fact that they were properly cared for when it came to shelter and diet. Nevertheless, the children appeared to "die from sadness."[2] Fast-forward to the 1930s and '40s in US hospitals, and the same phenomenon repeated itself. Children who should have survived were unable to do so. As psychiatrists attempted to put the puzzle pieces together, they determined the children who died were ones who appeared unable to relate to others. A brilliant man, John Bowlby, came along about this time and determined that what these children needed just as much as food, water, and shelter was genuine relationships with people who could support their emotional needs. The rest is history. Bowlby's theory of attachment remains among one of the most important scientific discoveries of all time.

I think it's pretty neat that a little Hebrew tribe in the ancient world knew about the theory of attachment long before Bowlby did, as revealed in the first pages of the Bible: We are not designed to navigate this world alone but in companionship with others. We are, by our very nature, social creatures. As the old African proverb said: If you want to go fast, go alone. If you want to go far, go together.

If you need further convincing, just ask one of the members of

Generation Z (those born between 1997 and approximately 2012,[3] according to Pew Research Center) who have reported being the loneliest generation in America. No surprise that they're also the most stressed out.[4]

I decided to start this book by being transparent with you about my own mental health struggles. Part of me wanted to write this book while keeping you at a distance from the most painful moments of my life. As a licensed therapist and ordained pastor, I could very well write to you about mental health and spirituality from the authority of my training and credentialing without baring my soul—but to do so felt dishonest and, frankly, less than helpful. Because while it may be true that I have some expertise in this arena, it is also true that I am a cosufferer. And I want you to know that someone who has not merely studied the valley but walked in its shadows penned every word you read in this book. Even though it makes me feel uncomfortable and vulnerable, I see sharing in this way as both helpful for you and a necessary step for my own healing. This is me choosing to believe you and I aren't alone in this; this is me following through with the truth that we are better together.

To know this truth, to be able to fight back against the lies and trust there's something good and beautiful and healing and filled with blessing beyond your current suffering, you'll have to choose to accept this for yourself. This is huge, so pay close attention. My telling you it's true won't do you much good. You have to believe it too.

Maybe for you, choosing to believe looks like pulling a friend aside and sharing the heaviness that has been on your heart. Maybe it means getting honest in your prayer life and begging God for grace and peace like you've never begged before. Maybe it means picking up the phone and making an appointment with a therapist. Maybe it means finally swallowing the pill your doctor prescribed for you. Whatever the case, however this looks for you, the key is moving slowly but deliberately into this truth as you make it your own. There is no other way.

It may very well be the most difficult thing you ever do. I'm asking you to do it anyway.

TOMORROW CAN BE DIFFERENT THAN TODAY

I understand, however, if, at this early stage in our journey together, you don't believe me when I say it can get better. At the height of my own depression, my mother, who has also courageously fought this disease for years, made me look her in the eyes while she promised me, "You will not always feel as bad as you do today. Things will change. You will feel better. Tomorrow can be very different than today." In that moment there was nothing I wanted more than to believe her. If she was wrong, then I honestly couldn't imagine a future. If every day was going to be as awful as that day and the days leading up to it, then there wouldn't be a way for me to move forward.

How could I live when I was so anxious I couldn't stop shaking? How could I take care of my own children when I was terrified at the prospect of my wife running to the grocery store, leaving me in charge? How could I enjoy anything if I couldn't sleep at night?

I couldn't answer those questions. Which meant something had to give. I could either choose to believe my mom and hold out hope for a better tomorrow or acquiesce to the pain of that day and give up.

By the grace of God, I chose to believe my mom.

I wrote this book because I want you to believe her too. And it starts with knowing you are not alone and reaching out for help. Remember, asking for help is never weakness, only strength.

MENTAL HEALTH: TRUE OR FALSE?

- In a given year, one in four American adults will experience a mental health condition.
- The United States suffers from a dramatic shortage of psychiatrists.
- Roughly twenty American veterans die by suicide every day, accounting for 14 percent of all suicides—though they represent only 8 percent of the population.
- Among people ages ten to thirty-four, suicide is the second-leading cause of death.
- By 2030, the annual global cost of mental disorders is projected to be $16 trillion, more than diabetes and cancer combined.
- More than seventy thousand Americans died from an opioid overdose in 2017.
- In 2013, one in six American adults reported taking some kind of mental health medication.
- Twenty-three percent of pastors have personally struggled with mental illness of some kind.
- Suicides and suicide attempts in the United States in 2013 cost the nation $58.4 million, though experts believe the actual cost was closer to $90 million due to underreporting.
- Men are roughly four times more likely to die by suicide than women.

- Only 41 percent of the Americans who had a mental disorder in 2018 received professional health care or other services.

True.[1]
All of them.
It hurts.
I know.

TWO

WHAT IS MENTAL HEALTH?

Before we can continue on in the healing journey, it would probably be helpful to understand what exactly mental health and mental illness are. Mental health and mental illness are two terms that often get used interchangeably, which I think is both confusing and helpful. It's confusing because drawing a hard line between mental health and illness is somewhat illusory in the sense that all health is best viewed on a continuum. After all, who can claim to be fully healthy in the mind or the body? Isn't the balance always in flux? Mine sure is. Just depends on the day.

The distinction is helpful, however, because there is obviously a difference between someone who suffers from a serious mental disorder like schizophrenia and a person who does not. Consequently, it seems worthwhile to parse out the two definitions, even if, at times, we allow some overlap in conversation. Let's look at mental health first.

DEFINING MENTAL HEALTH

The American Psychological Association (APA) says mental health is "the way your thoughts, feelings, and behaviors affect your life.

Good mental health leads to positive self-image and in turn, satisfying relationships with friends and others. Having good mental health helps you make good decisions and deal with life's challenges at home, work, or school."[1] I think that's a fair definition. There are many others out there, but let's work with this one for the time being. After all, the APA is the organization responsible for publishing the *Diagnostic and Statistical Manual of Mental Disorders* we talked about earlier (*DSM-5*), the authoritative guide to the diagnosis of mental disorders in the United States and much of the world. It is often referred to as the "Bible of psychiatry." So let's break down the APA's definition to get a good handle on what it means.

Mental health is the way your thoughts, feelings, and behaviors affect your life.

How we think affects how we feel, which in turn affects how we act. If we have overall positive, reasonable, and balanced thought lives, this will bleed over into every other area, enabling us to live happily, peacefully, and productively. If, however, our thought lives become warped by depression or anxiety, our thought patterns can turn toxic and infect every area, prohibiting our ability to find peace and enjoy rich relationships with others. *It's critical to understand that mental health is not so much affected by what happens to us as it is how we interpret what happens.* This is why two people can have the same experience but feel differently about it.

I hated flying on airplanes as a kid. My siblings, on the other hand, thought that blasting through the sky in a death tube attached to blazing rockets was nothing but a good time. Whenever we hit a patch of turbulence, they'd giggle with delight or throw up their arms as if riding on a roller coaster. My hands remained firmly clinched to my father's arm while he tried to assure me our violent deaths weren't imminent. We were all riding on the same airplane and experiencing the same turbulence. I interpreted the turbulence as a sign of danger and was thus scared by it. My siblings interpreted it as something that enhanced the ride and thus welcomed it—even hoped for it. It was the exact same event but with different interpretations, which led to different feelings and actions.

These days I fly without a care in the world other than securing an aisle seat because airplanes cause my bladder to magically revert to the size it was when I was born. But that's neither here nor there. The point is that turbulence no longer frightens me because I think differently about it. As a kid, the bumpy air was mysterious and felt like a signal that the plane was going to crash. Now I understand turbulence for what it is: a sudden change in airflow that signals nothing beyond the reality that the plane is flying through choppy air in the same way a boat glides over waves in the sea. It's all just part of the ride.

How we think affects how we feel, which affects how we act. Don't you forget it! This concept is critical not only for understanding mental health but also improving it.

Good mental health leads to positive self-image.

During one of my depressive episodes, I was unable to go to work and expressed to a friend how frustrating this was for me because not working made me feel worthless. I recounted how my kindergarten-aged son had, on his way out the door for school, asked me what time *I* left for work each day. His innocent question nearly brought me to my knees. It was all I could do to keep myself together until he left. When he did, I cried like the helpless person I believed I had become.

One of the hallmarks of mental illness, especially depression, is taking an overly negative view of oneself. A single setback, a minor mistake at work, or a relapse in symptoms can jumpstart a negative loop of self-defeating thoughts that make it very difficult, if not impossible, to gather an accurate self-image.

On the flipside, people who are mentally healthy know they are worthy of love and respect both from themselves and others, regardless of their circumstances. They implicitly understand that just because things aren't going well doesn't mean they can't see themselves as being well and that all human beings have inherent value. Recognizing this value allows them to see their own positive characteristics and talents as making them unique in this world, which further leads to feelings of self-worth.

For Christians, this means knowing we are loved unconditionally by the God of infinite grace and mercy who takes us in his arms and calls us his beloved children, simply because we exist. How different would your life be if you actually took that truth to heart?

Similar to God's, my son's love for me didn't depend on whether I was actually going to work that day. He wanted to ask a question about my life because he cared about my life. That, in and of itself, should have reminded me that I had value, but all I could focus on was the fact that I *wasn't* going to work, which in my mind meant I had no value. A mentally healthy person can receive the loving bids from others and allow those to help them see themselves as deeply cherished. After I recounted to my friend the exchange I had with my son, he said, "I have those days, too, Ryan. Days when I feel like nothing I do actually matters. Days when my job feels like a total joke. It's on those days I remind myself that Jesus Christ—*the Jesus Christ*—knows me and loves me. And you know what? That's enough. It's honestly enough for me."

Good mental health leads to a positive self-image by allowing us to feel the love of others and the love of God.

Good mental health leads to satisfying relationships with friends and others.

As we have already noted, human beings are designed for relationship, and thus we crave interpersonal connectedness from the moment we are born until the day we die. A mentally healthy person will seek out and maintain relationships with friends and others because it makes life more meaningful and exciting and provides the solace needed to deal with the more troubling times. When mental illness strikes, this desire to be close to others often fades away, and the person who is struggling begins to withdraw from loved ones, isolating in ways that tend to only heighten suffering. When I am unwell one of the hardest things for me is returning text messages from friends and family. The mere ping or vibration of my phone will give me anxiety because I just want to be left alone—which is the opposite of what I need. After all, what was the one thing in all of creation God said wasn't good?

You got it.

A psychiatrist recently told me that if he can get his patients struggling with addiction plugged into a healthy community then half the battle will be won. I take that to mean community is just as important, if not more important, than any amount of therapy and medication. In fact, community can be a preemptive strike to ward off mental illness much like a vaccine does with the flu. Research has shown a direct correlation between the size and strength of a person's support system and that person's likelihood to become depressed. People who indicate a low level of social support in their lives are significantly more likely to become depressed than people who say their social support system is robust and meaningful.

It's not just the number of friends a person has but the level of intimacy in those relationships that really makes a difference—a fact that we, living in the age of social media, understand all too well. At last check I had almost five thousand friends on Facebook. How ridiculous is that? I don't know five thousand people. And even if I did, trust me, I wouldn't ever want to or be able to talk to so many people. And I'm absolutely positive those people wouldn't want to talk to me!

It's not the number of people we know but the degree to which we know and are known that matters. Sadly, a recent poll of millennials found that more than one in four reported not having a single close friend.[2] An Ipsos poll of more than twenty thousand American adults discovered that nearly half always or sometimes feel lonely.[3] One in six also indicated they rarely or never feel as though they have close friends or family members who truly understand them. Statistics like these have led psychiatrists like Stephanie Cacioppo to declare that loneliness is an emerging public-health crisis.[4] When you consider that a study out of BYU found that loneliness is associated with a 26 percent jump in mortality risk, comments like Cacioppo's sound far from alarmist.[5] In fact, at 26 percent, loneliness is just as much a factor in people's deaths as smoking and obesity.

Good mental health promotes satisfying relationships. Similarly, it appears that a lack of satisfying relationships negatively affects mental health.

Good mental health helps you make good decisions.

Have you ever noticed how much harder it is to think when you're stressed versus when you're not? When I'm well rested and relaxed, I feel (wrongly) that I can do anything. My attitude is, *Bring it on, and I'll figure it out!* But get me tired enough or stressed out enough and I lose almost all confidence in my ability to do anything.

One time I married a couple who were having a very fancy black-tie wedding reception after the ceremony, which meant I needed to change out of my clerical clothing and into a tuxedo before driving to the country club. When the service ended, I hurriedly changed into the tux in my office and then hopped in the car with my wife, who drove while I tied my bow tie.

Or, I should say, tried to tie my bow tie.

This should have been no problem because, at this point, I had been wearing bow ties for years. I couldn't remember the last time I'd worn a regular necktie. But on this particular night I was stressed because during the ceremony I had mispronounced the name of the groom. I was terribly worried I had offended him and his family, with whom I was close. My brain shut down. I could not perform a simple task I had executed hundreds of times before. I must have tried to tie the bow tie twenty times during that drive, but no dice. I had no choice but to walk into that reception with the tie hanging around my neck as if I were leaving after a long night of partying. Stress bested me.

The feeling of diminished brain capacity when under stress is a universal condition to the human experience. The part of our brains responsible for our thoughts and actions, the prefrontal cortex, is also the most susceptible to the negative effects of stress. Put simply, the more stressed we are, the worse our prefrontal cortexes perform. Consequently, when mental health suffers, so does our ability to make good decisions. People who suffer from panic attacks will be the first to tell you that when the panic sets in, it can send their decision-making ability completely off-line. The only thing they can think about is getting the racing heart and chaotic thoughts to stop.

When a person suffers from a serious mental illness, the ability to make good decisions can often get warped by the symptoms of the condition, making bad decisions look like extraordinarily good ones. I recently spoke to a man with bipolar disorder who spent thousands of dollars purchasing books he didn't need while on vacation and in a manic state. Had he not been suffering from mania, he would have never made the decision to max out his credit card in such an irresponsible fashion. But because his mental health was compromised, so was his decision-making ability.

Good mental health allows the prefrontal cortex to function at maximum capacity, ensuring we have the ability to make good decisions.

Good mental health helps you deal with life's challenges at home, work, or school.

Resilience is often thought of as a characteristic belonging only to an extraordinary few people who overcome seemingly impossible situations. When I think of resilience, I think of people who do things I could never imagine doing. People like Victoria Arlen who spent four years "locked" in her own body, unable to move but fully aware of everything going on around her. Doctors gave her almost no chance of surviving the ordeal, much less of making any kind of meaningful recovery. Despite the odds, Victoria not only survived but also relearned how to eat and talk and walk. She went on to win three silver medals and one gold at the London 2012 Paralympic Games. Today she works as a television personality for ESPN and gives motivational speeches all over the world.

I think of Tom Brady winning a Super Bowl at the age of forty-one. I think of Stephen Hawking becoming the most important theoretical physicist since Albert Einstein while living with a motor-neuron disease that doctors said would kill him two years after his diagnosis at twenty-one. I think of J. K. Rowling writing Harry Potter while living in poverty. These are the people who come to mind when I think of resilience.

But resilience, according to the American Psychological Association, is far more ordinary than it is extraordinary. Resilience is not, in fact, a rare quality that certain people are born with but, rather, it is made up of thoughts, feelings, and actions that can be learned by anyone. And most people *do* learn them and use them in their daily lives.

Consider how the majority of people respond to major tragedies like 9/11 or Hurricane Katrina. When faced with tragedy, by and large, people are quick to gather themselves and, with resiliency, begin rebuilding what was lost, often coming back even stronger and better than they were before. Consequently, a sign of good mental health is a person's ability to hit life's curveballs. When things don't go as planned, how do they respond? Are they quick to rise to the challenge by looking for alternative solutions, or are they all too ready to throw in the towel, convinced they are ill-equipped to do what needs to be done? When tragedy strikes or trauma is suffered or divorce is filed, what happens then? If a person is in good mental health, they will display resilience and be able to bounce back from the setback. If a person's mental health is suffering, however, their ability to display resilience will be compromised.

When facing a tragedy, people in poor mental health are far more prone to catastrophize or engage in all-or-nothing thinking. So the towers fall down on 9/11, and instead of looking to help others or reimagining a new life in the wake of the destruction, they see the tragedy as insurmountable. Terrorists struck once, which means life can never be the same. It also means it's only a matter of time until it happens again, but this time it will be much worse. A person in poor mental health catches a cold and worries about cancer. A relationship ends, and they're convinced they'll be alone forever.

Good mental health allows a person to demonstrate the enormous capacity of the human spirit to not shrink when faced with a challenge but rise to meet it with strength, brilliance, and resolve.

MY DEFINITION

While it's preferable to trust authorities like the APA over folks like me, I do have another simple way of thinking about mental health that I've found helpful when trying to make sense of it. Mental health is the little voice inside your head that's been talking to you for as long as you can remember. You know it really well, even if you've never taken the time to fully acknowledge its presence in your life.

It sounds just like you. You're the only one who can hear it. And it's more convincing to you than anything or anyone else in the entire world. Which is why it wields such an enormous power over your life and also why it's critical that you care for it every day of your life.

Some days you wake up and the voice is kind and loving, intent on encouraging you through difficult circumstances. Other times it reminds you that you're safe and it's totally okay to relax and soak up the small pleasures in life, freeing you up to notice a beautiful sunset or enjoy the laughter of a child. Whatever it says, you listen because you know it's coming from within you, a place you can trust. It is, quite literally, *you talking to you.*

From the moment we became self-aware of our existence, we began hearing this voice inside our heads, making the human experience one in which we not only live but also reflect on our living. Put simply: we think about our own thinking.

Dogs don't do this. Our iPhones don't do this (at least not yet). Nor do fish, enchiladas, or trees for that matter. Some folks think computers might eventually do this via artificial intelligence, but the jury's still out on that one. The truth is that no living creature is self-aware in the way we humans are. This kind of existence appears to be wholly unique to those of us described in the Bible as having been created in the image of God. We move and live and have our being in a body with a brain that partners with a soul to produce our mind. Our mental health, then, refers to the complex interactions between mind, body, and soul that either work to create inner peace or distress. Put another way, mental health is the foundation of our overall health.

And it's not just the absence of mental illness, a point the World Health Organization (WHO) picks up on nicely in its definition of mental health. WHO says, "Mental health is a state of well-being in which an individual realizes his or her own abilities, can cope with the normal stresses of life, can work productively and is able to make a contribution to his or her community."[6]

Mental health is the voice inside your head.

Call it the brain.

Call it the work of the brain.

Call it the mind.

Call it the soul.

Call it your inner Beyoncé.

Call it whatever you want.

Just, please, don't call it unimportant.

MENTAL HEALTH MATTERS

Regardless of how we choose to define mental health, its importance in our lives cannot be overstated. Mental health is critical for optimal living at every life stage and is always at risk of falling into illness if not cared for properly. Unfortunately, in the Christian community this is a statement that requires added emphasis.

For reasons we'll dive into later in the book, mental health and mental illness have too often been sidelined in the church. What I hope to highlight in this book, however, is that mental health is critical for spiritual health. For now, I'll just say this: as Christians we see ourselves not simply as bodies but bodies with souls. God created each of us to be a mysterious comingling of body and soul, of matter and spirit. This means that our mental health, our physical health, and our spiritual health are not three distinct aspects of our identities but rather three different expressions of our single identity. In the same way every Christian is a member of the single body of Christ, our three expressions of health are tied to the singular body we call our own. Consequently, the health of one inevitably affects the health of the others and vice versa. This being the case, our mental health must be seen as an integral part of what it means to be fully human and of what is needed for us to take the great Christian journey back toward God.

THREE

WHAT IS MENTAL ILLNESS?

Working to understand and treat mental illness has proven an enormous challenge for as long as society has existed. Even today, with our advanced forms of treatment and commitment to respecting the dignity of all people, we continue to struggle mightily with the stigma associated with mental illness in large part because we have failed to educate one another as to what mental illness actually is. Consequently, outside of the world of mental health care, the mentally ill continue to be largely misunderstood, marginalized, and often feared.

For example, many people believe the mentally ill are more prone to violence than others. This is why every time the gun control debate heats up you hear voices calling for restricted access for those with any kind of clinical diagnosis. It doesn't help that Hollywood has perpetuated this myth for decades. The reality, however, is that the mentally ill are far more likely to be victims of violence than perpetrators of it. How might knowing this affect the way you feel the next time you walk past a homeless person who is aggressively talking aloud to someone who clearly only exists in his mind? If you understand the odds of him attacking you are very low, might you be less likely to cross the street and more inclined to slow down and offer a smile and even a prayer? Anytime we can remove fear from a situation, a new host of possibilities appears.

It's not just those who suffer severely and require hospitalization who are misunderstood but also those of us who count ourselves among the one out of every four Americans who battle their mental health each and every year. These are the silent sufferers. These are your bankers, lawyers, stay-at-home moms, pastors, students, bakers, doctors, and artists. These are the high-functioning folks who show up to work, live in nice houses, and volunteer in their communities. These are the people who do everything they're supposed to do without anyone around them ever having a clue about the internal battles they are fighting.

A beautiful and intelligent young woman with a high-powered job sat crying in my office recently, trying to stave off a terrible panic, when she blurted out, "I honestly just wish I had cancer or something. That way maybe somebody would understand my pain. At least that way I would know it was either going to improve or kill me! But these," she pointed to her head, "these gremlins who talk to me, are they ever going to stop? And am I ever going to not feel so totally alone?"

This woman's sentiments capture perfectly what so many of us who struggle with our mental health feel. The pain is so intense we desire almost any other malady to take its place. And often the people closest to us either can't or haven't taken the time to truly understand what it is we are experiencing. In an effort to help bridge the gap between those who suffer and those who don't, let's turn now to a discussion of what mental illness is. Or, I should say, what we believe it to be.

In his wonderful book, *Good Reasons for Bad Feelings*, evolutionary psychiatrist Randolph M. Neese recounted an exchange he had when interviewing for medical school in 1969. When asked what kind of physician he hoped to become, Neese replied that he wanted to train as a psychiatrist. Upon hearing this the interviewer asked, "Why would you want to do that? They're going to find the brain causes for mental disorders soon, and it will all become neurology."[1]

Welp.

It's 2021 and that ain't happened.

To date, there is no way to diagnose mental disorders in the same way doctors do with other diseases. There is no blood test for depression. No genetic screening for anxiety. And while many alcoholics describe their brains as being broken, fMRI scans of the brain have yet to show how that might actually be the case.

Given these realities, how should we define mental illness? Is it a disease or a disorder in the brain? And if so, what is the difference between a disease and a disorder anyway? Does disease refer to something biological and disorder to something psychological? Or is it the other way around?

Bring these questions up with psychiatrists, psychologists, and other mental health professionals and you'll hear a plethora of answers. When a person breaks a leg, doctors can determine how and why the bone broke as it did and more or less what to do in order to mend it back together quickly and effectively. When it comes to mental illness, however, this task is exponentially harder because we get sick and recover from mental illness in many different ways, some of which continue to befuddle both physicians and therapists alike.

It would be lovely if there were a simple and standard explanation for mental illness. But there isn't one. Any person who tells you otherwise is either ignorant to the history and complexity of this issue or lying.

Currently, the medical model (which governs our system of managed care) defines mental disorders as brain diseases, which in some cases is verifiably true. For example, the brains of patients with Alzheimer's often exhibit abnormalities upon postmortem examination. Likewise, some patients with bipolar disorder and autism also show differences in their brains, albeit mostly small and inconsistent. More recently, the brains of football players like Junior Seau and Aaron Hernandez, who died by suicide, have shown signs of chronic traumatic encephalopathy (CTE), a progressive brain disease that results from too much trauma to the brain. So, yes, mental illness involves brain disease, but is that the sum total of the explanation?

No. Not even close.

Even those who subscribe to the medical model of mental illness acknowledge it can rarely be boiled down to one single cause. In most cases, it comes about from a confluence of factors that involve our biology, our psychology, and our environment. This is why the *DSM-5* defines mental illness as "a syndrome characterized by clinically significant disturbance in an individual's cognition, emotion regulation, or behavior that reflects a dysfunction in the psychological, biological, or developmental processes underlying mental functioning."[2]

Casting all mental disorders as diseases has proven an underwhelming definition because it's simply too reductionist in nature. For instance, some mental illnesses result from a person being at the far end of the spectrum of a normally distributed trait, such as a low IQ. Having a low IQ is certainly a disadvantage in life, but are we really prepared to say that person has a disease? What about a soldier who watches his best friends die on the field of battle and returns home with PTSD? Is he diseased for struggling to make sense of the horrors of war? Or is it more accurate to say he is a human being with deep and complex feelings that sometimes can't be managed without professional assistance? The same can be asked of victims of sexual assault. Is the disease model nuanced enough to capture what's going on with the mental state of a woman who has been raped and is now suffering from insomnia and panic attacks?

When a patient comes down with pneumonia, doctors can usually locate the bacteria that brought about the condition. Not so with hoarding, claustrophobia, or depression. So while it may be true that these disorders are in fact diseases, it is also true that they are labeled as such *not* by biological evidence but rather by clusters of symptoms. Put simply: we diagnose mental illness mostly by observing behavior as opposed to running tests in the lab.

That said, observing behavior is far from an objective task. Scientists and therapists vary wildly in how they understand appropriate causes and treatments of mental illness, as Dr. Neese succinctly explained:

Doctors who look for hereditary factors and brain disorders recommend drugs. Therapists who blame early experience and mental conflicts recommend psychotherapy. Clinicians who focus on learning suggest behavior therapy. Those who focus on distorted thinking recommend cognitive therapy. Therapists with a religious orientation suggest meditation and prayer. And therapists who believe most problems arise from family dynamics usually recommend, predictably, family therapy.[3]

Are you beginning to see the challenge?

Adding to the complexity of defining mental illness is the reality that when we talk about it, we are not just talking about a *state of being* but actual *human beings* who, for most of history, have suffered mightily because of their battles with mental health. Let's not forget that it was in recent history that the primary solution for dealing with the mentally ill in this country was to simply lock them up in insane asylums. Nor can we ignore the fact that America's current largest mental health provider is Cook County Jail in Chicago, where one in three inmates suffers from some form of mental illness.[4] Consequently, any discussion we have about mental illness must take place with painstaking sensitivity.

As a Christian I feel an especially strong duty to do everything in my power to not further magnify the stigma and misunderstanding that cause additional pain to those who suffer. Mental illness is tough enough without any added shame.

Thus, for our purposes, let's define mental illness very simply by saying it is *any* persistently harmful thoughts, feelings, or actions.

UNDERSTANDING MENTAL ILLNESS

As we have already discussed, mental illnesses are commonly understood as diseases and thus need to be diagnosed on the basis of symptoms and treated with therapy, medication, or a combination of both. But the disease model alone does not provide a comprehensive enough picture for understanding mental illness. To gain a fuller understanding, we must undertake what is called the biopsychosocial approach, in which we look at the biological, psychological, and social factors that can lead to mental illness.

Biological

I have yet to meet a person with an uncomplicated relationship to their body. I know I don't have one. I was once standing in a crowded casino lobby in Vegas when I noticed a perfect stranger staring at my feet, which were in sandals. "Your feet," she said, pointing at them. "They're really small." I don't wear sandals anymore.

In ninth grade, one of my classmates (a girl I had a crush on) tapped me on the shoulder. "Your face," she said, "your cheeks, it's like you stuffed food in them. They're puffy." *Right*, I thought. *So I guess you're not asking me to Sadie Hawkins?*

As a kid I dreaded the moment at Christmas when some uncle would lift me in the air and say, "When ya gonna put some meat on those bones?" Looking back, I wish I'd had the courage to respond, "Never! I am never putting meat on these bones because it's physically impossible. And that's A-OK."

But I didn't say any of that because I was a kid with small feet, puffy cheeks, and no meat. And all of it made me feel bad. All of it hurt.

I think it's safe to say that a good number of us have less than healthy mental states when it comes to our bodies. But it's not just an issue of how we feel about our bodies. It's also an issue of how our bodies, or our biology, can physically contribute to mental illness. There are two biological influences that are of particular importance in this: genetics and brain chemistry.

Some psychiatrists argue that every major psychiatric disorder has a heritable component.[5] Whether this is true remains to be seen, but scientists have long recognized that many psychiatric disorders run in families, suggesting potential genetic roots. This is why mental health professionals insist on gathering a good family history for their patients. If, for example, schizophrenia, bipolar disorder, or substance use disorder has been prevalent in a person's family of origin, it could very well mean the patient has inherited certain genetic traits that would increase susceptibility to the disease. People with parents or siblings who report having depression are up to five times as likely to experience the illness themselves.[6] While no single gene has been discovered to cause depression or any other type of mental illness, there does seem to be evidence that genetics play a role.

Brain chemistry is the other biological factor at play with mental illness. Since our brains are necessarily involved in every action of our bodies, it stands to reason that brain functioning would also affect mental health. But brains are mega complicated (to put it mildly), and the exact nature of how our most complex organ influences our mental health remains one of life's great mysteries. That said, we know that a person's mental health can deteriorate as a result of a chemical imbalance in the brain.

The story goes something like this: neurons in the brain communicate with one another via chemical messengers called neurotransmitters. In order for the brain to function optimally, the levels of various neurotransmitters need to be properly maintained. Consequently, if a person's brain runs a deficit of a specific neurotransmitter, mental health problems might arise. Not everyone buys this story hook, line, and sinker, but it's widely considered to be pretty darn good science.

While you may not be familiar with the term *neurotransmitter*, you most likely know a few of them by name. Does *dopamine*, *GABA*, or *serotonin* ring a bell? Dopamine makes the news a lot because it is responsible for that rush of excitement you feel when social media notifications blaze up your phone. GABA helps you calm down when frightened. And serotonin, the biggie, helps regulate your entire life—mood, social behavior, sexual desire, memory, and sleep. So when our brains are out of balance with any of these neurotransmitters, it can lead to mental illness.

Psychological

One of the main factors most people think of when talking about mental illness is, of course, psychology, or our thoughts. Our thoughts have an almost infinite power to influence the quality of mental health. Everything comes back to the stories we tell ourselves.

On a sunny afternoon in Los Angeles when I was in college, I went to swim laps at the university pool. When I returned home an hour or so later, I noticed, from afar, that a motorcycle was parked in my driveway. Being a self-centered twenty-year-old, my first thought was, *I can't believe my parents bought me a motorcycle!* I picked up the pace but, as I got closer, noticed something strange about the bike. There was a man sitting on it, decked out in all black leather, helmet on, but slumped over as if sleeping. My second thought was, *Why is this strange man taking a nap on my new bike?*

"Hello?" I said.

The man robotically sat up, turned toward me, and began to slowly lift the helmet visor shielding his face. My third thought was, *This guy's gonna kill me. Why didn't I realize he's obviously a hit man sent to take me out?*

"Hi, Ryan," my father said, smiling wide.

In a matter of what could have, at most, been two minutes, I went from thinking I had a new bike to being terrified that I was going to die at the hands of the person on said new bike to ultimately feeling relieved to see my father who had surprised me in California on *his* bike.

One event.

Three stories.

Three *very* different feelings.

Our thoughts have enormous power.

Consider the following scene: You're walking down the hallway at work and you pass your boss who is walking the other way while looking down at his phone. You offer a quick hello, but your boss says nothing in reply.

How do you feel in this moment?

What thoughts are running through your head?

However you're feeling is going to depend on what you're thinking. If you're having a great day and thinking about how competent you are at your job, you're likely to assume your boss was simply distracted by whatever he was looking at on his phone. The snub wasn't intentional. You carry on without thinking about the incident. Your thoughts are preoccupied in a healthy way, on things like planning for an upcoming conference call, and you move on quickly from the scene.

But if you're having a less-than-stellar day, wondering about whether you're cut out for this line of work, you may interpret the snub from your boss entirely differently. You might begin to think about *all* the times your boss has been rude to you and conclude he doesn't like you. Maybe he's avoiding you because he's preparing to fire you and feels awkward whenever he sees you in the hallway. Or maybe you're so insignificant to him that he doesn't feel the need to acknowledge your presence. Suddenly, you feel anxious and stressed and can't focus on planning for that upcoming conference call.

Our thoughts affect our feelings, then our feelings affect the thoughts that follow, and on and on it goes. Mental health professionals call this the ABC model of thinking.

A psychologist named Albert Ellis invented the model. If you've never heard of Ellis, I highly recommend you look him up on YouTube. He is simultaneously the funniest and most terrifying therapist I have ever seen. While I love his insights, I don't think I'd have been brave enough to actually pay him money to insult me. He invented a form of psychotherapy called rational emotive behavior therapy, which is designed to challenge irrational thinking. He was famous for telling clients they mostly made up depression in their own heads, which meant they were capable of unmaking it. He also attributed much of a person's anxiety to an obsession over reputation. Like I said, Ellis wasn't for everyone, but his insights into how powerfully our thoughts affect our feelings can't be denied.

Here's how the ABC model works:

- **The A stands for the activating event.** These are the so-called facts of any given situation. You can think of the A as what you might see if a camera had literally recorded the event. This is what many would describe as the objective truth.
- **The B stands for the belief about the activating event.** As Ellis pointed out, we are often not actively aware of the belief we attach to the event, instead accepting our belief as the truth of the event itself. Our belief is whatever "running story" we attach to the event.
- **The C stands for the consequences.** This is our reaction to A and B as expressed in emotion, physiology, or behavior.

What typically happens is that we are aware of A and C but fail to appreciate the role of B. In other words, we believe the situation caused our reaction—be it negative or positive—when in fact it was most likely our interpretation, our thoughts about the situation, that had the most to do with the consequences.

Here's a very simple example of how this works: Let's say my wife is out of town and it's up to me to make sure my two sons are fed, bathed, and put in bed on time so they are rested and ready to successfully face the coming day. But none of this happens as it should because when I get home from work, I'm exhausted and short-tempered, which means I don't get dinner on the table in time. Consequently, I hurry the boys through dinner, throw them in a lukewarm bath, and scurry them into their beds without brushing their teeth or reading them bedtime stories, all the while being snippy and emotionally unavailable. (I swear this is just hypothetical.)

So, the *activating event* is that I didn't get the boys to bed on time. My *belief* is that I'm a bad father. And the *consequence* is that I feel depressed about it. If, however, I choose to employ the ABC model of thinking, I can reframe this event and produce a very different consequence. For example, there is no real evidence to suggest that, just because I was unable to get my boys to bed on time, I am a bad father. The reality is that I did the best I could under the circumstances. Yes, it would have been great if I would have come home earlier and in a better mood. This, no doubt, would have helped me accomplish the tasks on time and in a healthier fashion. But failing to do so hardly justifies my self-judgment that I am now a bad father. And if I'm not a bad father, then what, exactly, am I depressed about?

See how it works?

The problem with mental illness and thinking, however, is that we don't recognize our irrational thoughts and often find ourselves locked in never-ending loops of negative thoughts that cause us to spiral downward.

If you've ever experienced these sorts of thoughts, please remember you're far from alone. In 1980 Philip Kendall and Steven

Hollon made a list of thirty thoughts they heard their depressed patients express to them:

1. I feel like I'm up against the world.
2. I'm no good.
3. Why can't I ever succeed?
4. No one understands me.
5. I've let people down.
6. I don't think I can go on.
7. I wish I were a better person.
8. I'm so weak.
9. My life's not going the way I want it to.
10. I'm so disappointed in myself.
11. Nothing feels good anymore.
12. I can't stand this anymore.
13. I can't get started.
14. What's wrong with me?
15. I wish I were somewhere else.
16. I can't get things together.
17. I hate myself.
18. I'm worthless.
19. Wish I could just disappear.
20. What's the matter with me?
21. I'm a loser.
22. My life is a mess.
23. I'm a failure.
24. I'll never make it.
25. I feel so helpless.
26. Something has to change.
27. There must be something wrong with me.

28. My future is bleak.
29. I'm just not worth it.
30. I can't finish anything.[7]

When I'm doing well, I can read that list and easily see how misguided these thoughts are. But when I'm depressed, many of these exact thoughts cycle endlessly through my brain, doing nothing but making me feel worthless and even more depressed. Distorted thinking feels like you've invited a critic who hates you to take up residence in your brain and scream at you all day and all night long. It doesn't make any logical sense and yet there it is. It's no surprise that our thoughts play such a role in mental illness.

Sociological

As we all know, however, even the most clearheaded thinker among us can still struggle with mental health. That's because we do not live in this world as independent thinking beings but are interconnected to everything and everyone around us. So, while rational thinking might take us a long way toward good mental health, there are still a lot of other factors ready and willing to throw us off course.

Our social existence refers to the large bucket of activities, circumstances, and relationships that stitch together the fabric of our lives. This includes our emotions, interpersonal relationships with family and friends, spirituality, cultural influences, socioeconomic status, political affiliation, and trauma. This list could go on, in theory, forever. The basic idea is that our mental health will always be affected by the world we live in, which is another way of saying that mental health does not exist within the vacuum of any one individual.

Certain life experiences can trigger a mental illness or, at the very least, contribute to its development. When it comes to mental illness, we refer to these sorts of events as risk factors. Rarely does a risk factor present itself as a single incident—although it can in instances of sexual assault or other forms of trauma—but rather multivariate experiences that influence in any untold number of ways. While not exhaustive, some of the more common risk factors for mental illness include:

- Abuse
- Addiction
- Chronic illness
- Divorce
- Family violence
- Poverty
- Trauma
- Loneliness
- Illiteracy
- Learning difficulties
- Pessimism
- Poor diet
- Being an overburdened caregiver
- Sexual assault
- Terminal illness
- Having a family member or spouse with a severe mental illness

Experiencing or being exposed to any one of the circumstances on the list above does not, by any means, predetermine mental illness, but it's good to be aware that these scenarios can raise the risk of suffering from a mental health challenge.

The power our social lives have over mental health comes into further focus when you realize that, while certain mental illnesses—like depression and schizophrenia—are prevalent around the world, others are not. Anorexia and bulimia, for example, are almost entirely Western illnesses, which is most likely correlated to Western media's obsession with extremely thin women. Moreover, clients from different ethnic backgrounds who live in the same country often experience mental illness in diverse ways, requiring diverse treatments by clinicians who understand the significance of cultural differences. For instance, Native Americans often see mental illness as a byproduct of disharmony with nature whereas Asian Americans are inclined to see mental illness as resulting from disharmony in family relationships.[8] As you can see, where we live and with whom we live not only affects how we get sick but also the means by which we hope to get better.

As Christians we ought to be keenly aware of how our lives affect one another. The Bible goes to great lengths to describe our relationships with one another as body parts of a single, whole body. Everything we do and say has the power to bring life or death, physically and spiritually, to the people with whom we are connected. When it comes to mental illness, what we say and do often is a life or death situation.

At the end of the day, it's imperative we recognize that mental illness can be brought about by any number of factors because it reminds us that anybody, at any time, can fall ill. No one is immune.

Jason Kander realized he wasn't immune in 2018 when he, a military hero and rising political star poised to become the next mayor of Kansas City, ended his campaign at the eleventh hour to tend to his increasing struggles with PTSD and depression. Despite the fact that he had landed a big book deal and was almost guaranteed elected office, Jason found himself on the phone with the VA suicide hotline. Even though he feared the stigma that would undoubtedly follow, he chose to seek help instead of victory. "I'm done hiding this from myself and from the world," he said.[9] Had Jason refused to acknowledge the seriousness of his condition he might have become mayor, but at what price? Thank God he understood that no amount of worldly success inoculates a person from mental illness. When it strikes it must be attended to with everything we have, no matter the cost. The stakes are too high. Jason may not have won that election, but he took home a prize far greater: his life.

What is mental illness?

A disease we must work hard to understand and talk about loudly so people like Jason Kander don't have to risk their lives trying to keep it hidden.

Oh, and guess what? At the time of this writing, Jason is once again healthy and thriving working for the Veterans Community Project, an organization that provides transitional housing for homeless veterans. He also has a podcast that debuted at number one on iTunes and a *New York Times* bestselling book. If mental illness ever tries to convince you that your life is over, please remember Jason and know that you have no idea what tomorrow might bring. But you have to be here tomorrow to find out what that might be.

So be here, friend.

FOUR

WHY DOES GOD ALLOW MENTAL ILLNESS?

It strikes me as one of the more unfair aspects of life that some people spend their days tormented by their own minds while others are permitted peaceful existences, unfettered by feelings of worthlessness and despair. When comparing the life of one who suffers from depression with one who doesn't, it's plain to see the one without the disorder has certain advantages. Why would God allow this painful illness? Why does he allow suffering at all?

I'll never forget a 911 recording I listened to a few years back. A man with diabetes was due to return to the hospital the next day to undergo an amputation. He had already lost one leg. Having made the decision to die rather than lose another limb, he attempted suicide. He shot himself in the head, but he survived, blinding himself in the process. Then he called 911 for help, asking to be taken to the very place he had tried desperately to avoid. The audio of the phone call is one of the saddest human exchanges I've ever heard.

The man tells the operator that he has shot himself in the head, the temple to be exact, but that it didn't work. When the operator asks if it was an accident, the man clearly states it was done in an intentional effort to avoid going to the hospital. The operator asks where the gun is now, and the man replies that it's beside him on the bed, although he is unable to open his eyes to see it. The conversation proceeds with the man describing his awful situation in more graphic detail so the operator can get him the help he needs. The call, however, ends with the police storming into the room and treating the man very harshly, as I assume they must, given the potentially dangerous situation he's put them in.

It is one of the saddest scenes I can imagine. A man decides to die by suicide to avoid a medical procedure. That in and of itself breaks my heart. How many unimaginable scenes like this one have played out over the course of human history? How many suicides? How many abuses? How many genocides? How many rapes? How many injustices? How many young girls and boys trafficked for sex? How many instances of suffering are occurring at this very moment? It trips the mind. Just the other night I read of a murder-suicide where a man was so convinced both he and his fiancée would test positive for COVID-19 that he ended their lives. The coroner later determined that neither one of them had the disease.

Why does God allow for these atrocities? What's the point of all the death and destruction? *Was there seriously not a better way to go about this, God?*

(Sigh.)

I wish I had a better answer to all of these questions that speaks to the larger question of why God allows suffering.

I've heard all the biblical arguments:

God allows suffering so we might learn to trust him. This seems to be the message of John chapter 9 when the disciples asked Jesus about the cause of the blind man's sin. They wanted to know whose sin it was that caused the blindness. Was it the man's or his parents' (v. 2)? Jesus said that neither sinned. The man was born blind simply so God's works might be revealed in him (v. 3).

Pretty tough to swallow, but okay.

God allows suffering because he uses it as a form of punishment for sin. I really have trouble with this one, but the psalmists often expressed just this kind of sentiment:

- "There is no soundness in my flesh because of your indignation; there is no health in my bones because of my sin. For my iniquities have gone over my head; like a heavy burden, they are too heavy for me." (Ps. 38:3–4 ESV)
- "LORD, be merciful to me; heal my soul, for I have sinned against You." (Ps. 41:4 NKJV)
- Paul also echoed this theology in the first chapter of Romans when he said that God hands us over to our sins and the subsequent suffering that inevitably follows (vv. 18–32).

God allows suffering so we might learn to be humble. This seems to be one of the lessons from the book of Job. When Job finally asked God near the end of the book why he had to endure so much suffering, God went off on the longest monologue we have from him in the entire Bible. His message? He is God and Job is not.

There are more arguments.

You've heard them all. But I suspect that you, like me, have trouble actually believing them. Not in the sense that they don't control truth, but more in the sense that they don't get at the whole truth—the truth that really matters, the one with the potential to redeem our suffering by helping us make sense of it.

Life is hard and full of suffering.

This much is certainly true.

But for what good?

What is the purpose for so much pain and strife? I have to think there are other ways God could have come up with to teach us humility or repentance or trust. God could just as easily do so through his beauty as through our pain. So why?

There is at least one argument that I find compelling:

Pain and suffering are useful for keeping us alive. We rarely make an appointment with a doctor because we are certain we have a disease. Rather, we experience some kind of discomfort or pain that prompts us to make an appointment to investigate what is causing the pain. This is often true with mental health. We must remember that symptoms are not the disorder but signs that let us know the disorder is up to something. In this respect, a low mood or a sudden loss of energy can be helpful when seen as a signal that something deeper is amiss within us. The symptoms of depression can work as warning signs, letting us know of danger ahead. Viewed through this lens, suffering at least takes on a functional role in our lives.

Have a bad headache? Might want to look into that. Could be a tumor.

Can't put weight on your left leg? Probably worth an X-ray. Leg might be broken.

And so on.

But still, I'm unsatisfied.

There has got to be more to this equation than the idea that physical suffering gives us a head start on fighting disease.

SO, WHAT IS THE PURPOSE OF SUFFERING?

I once worked with a man who started limping around the office one day. He had tripped during a recent half-marathon and thought his ankle was just taking longer than usual to recover. But then he started to trip when walking down the hallway and couldn't keep his balance when leaning over the fountain for a drink of water. One time he walked into my office to deliver a letter and fell forward as if he'd been shoved hard from behind. He was flustered and embarrassed, and I felt awful for him. Within months he had his diagnosis.

ALS.

For the next nine months he trekked into work while the disease went about its nasty work inside his body. It wasn't long before he needed a walker to get a drink from the water fountain. In less than one year's time, he went from running half marathons to moving as slowly and robotically as any person I've ever seen. It was devastating to watch. What must it have been like to live through?

Soon thereafter, at barely forty years old, he was forced to retire. The week he left the office for the last time, one of my colleagues observed that this man was now "going home to face his cross." Everyone in the room gave solemn nods of agreement. I just stood there thinking, *This is so unfair.*

And it was.

And it is.

He died a short time later.

I hand-fed him a meal a few weeks before his death, and I have never seen a more ravaging disease in my life. The kind of physical suffering this man endured was beyond my comprehension. I wouldn't wish this form of death on my worst enemy.

You know other stories like this one. Perhaps you've even lived one or are living one right now. As I write these words, my phone is pinging with news updates that Kobe Bryant, his thirteen-year-old daughter, and seven other people have perished in a helicopter crash. *What?* On average, twenty-five thousand people die of starvation each day.[1] *Are you kidding me?* A client of mine is currently facing charges of aggravated assault. If she receives time in prison, she's decided she'd rather die by suicide than face imprisonment. *Please, no.*

Why is this the world we live in?

The best answer I can find is the one revealed in the first pages of Genesis when God created humans and made them distinct from other creatures in a very particular manner: he gave us freedom.

God told Adam and Eve that they could have their run of the garden of Eden. They had total dominion over the land and could do as they saw fit with only one exception: They were not to eat the fruit from the Tree of the Knowledge of Good and Evil. But you know the story. They did just that, demonstrating in that moment what has been and remains true for all of humanity: we have the freedom to choose what we do in this life.

God, apparently, loves freedom. And since God created humanity in his own image, it must necessarily be the case that we, too, are free and designed to love and explore our freedom. Unlike the beasts of the earth who operate by instinct, we humans can choose to resist our instincts and make decisions by using more complex moral constructs, like right and wrong, to make decisions. If we were unable to veer away from good, we would not be truly free.

Could God have set this whole affair up differently? Of course. God is God, and God can do whatever God wants to do. But this is what God *has* done. This is the world we live in, and this is the world we must learn to make sense of if we are to find some semblance of peace within the suffering.

But what about mental illness when there is no choice involved? I can understand that God did not will Hitler to murder millions of Jewish people but rather that Hitler and others like him were the cause of that immeasurable suffering. But what about brain abnormalities that cause perfectly kind people to believe the trees in the park are trying to eat them? And what about mothers who give birth to their children and want nothing more than to hold and care for them but are stricken so hard by postpartum depression they must be readmitted to the hospital and kept away from the babies they just carried for nine months? How does God's love for freedom help us to make sense of this kind of suffering?

Again, I wish I had a better answer for you, but the best I can find also comes from Genesis.

From the moment Adam and Eve made the decision to stray away from God's intentional plans for life on earth, nothing has been the same. And this includes our bodies and the illnesses that plague them. I want to be careful here. I am not suggesting that illnesses are God's way of punishing humans but that they are simply another reality of our living in a fallen world. Mental illness is not the fault of any one individual but rather a disappointing reality for what it means to live life on this earth. Should I say it again, just in case?

Mental illness is not a punishment. It is just one of the gnarly waves of suffering we humans ride in this thing called life.

To accept this mindset requires a certain deference and humility toward God, for it could be easy to stamp our feet and demand that it ought not to be so. We want to say, God should have done this! God should have done that! God should have done better! But then, where would that get us? As Job learned, we are not God. And we cannot undo what God has already done. This brand of humility is exemplified quite beautifully in the words from a survivor of Auschwitz:

> It never occurred to me to question God's doing or lack of doings while I was an inmate at Auschwitz, although of course, I understand others did. . . . I was no less or no more religious because of what the Nazis did to us; and I believe my faith in God was not undermined in the least. It just never occurred to me to associate the calamity we were experiencing with God, to blame Him, or to believe in Him less or to cease believing in Him at all because He didn't come to our aid.
>
> God doesn't owe us that. Or anything. We owe our lives to Him. If someone believes God is responsible for the death of six million because He didn't somehow do something to save them, he's got his thinking reversed. We owe God our lives for the few or many years we live, and we have the duty to worship Him and do all that He commands us. That's what we're here on this earth for, to be in God's service, to do God's bidding.[2]

There is something to this. It is hard to swallow, for sure, but there is a deep truth in these words. If our purpose in life is to journey back to God and become fully human along the way, then, yes, we must oppose suffering at every opportunity; but to find ourselves stuck in an existential crisis over the nature of this existence is to miss the boat entirely. The point, as a Christian, is not to eradicate all suffering or even overcome suffering but to endure it faithfully and ease it in people and places when we are able to do so, as Jesus did. All of this makes it a little easier for me to swallow the reality of mental illness.

I think.

I hope.

What helps the most, however, is the image of Jesus Christ on the cross. The truth is that I'm not sure I could worship a God who hadn't tasted the bitterness of the kind of suffering we humans experience on a daily basis, especially those of us who suffer in the mind. But when I look at the cross, I see a God so intent on loving and living with his people that he was willing to crawl into the deepest pit of suffering known to humanity so all of humanity might know there is no darkness into which he will not give chase.

During one of my particularly brutal battles with depression and misuse of alcohol, I went away for in-patient rehab in California. As you can imagine, when I first got there, I was in a very dark place. I had not only hurt a lot of people on my way there, but being there now meant I had left my wife at home to care for our two sons alone while also fielding countless calls from friends and onlookers who were wanting to know what was going on with me. Why had Ryan suddenly disappeared? The guilt I felt was so overwhelming, I was all but certain it would take me under.

On one of the worst nights during treatment, I hid away in my room and read from Elie Wiesel's book *Night*. I had always wanted to read this book but had never taken the time to do so. Going to rehab has its perks, I suppose. Anyway, once I started reading, I couldn't stop. One of the passages that wedged into my heart that night, which I have never forgotten, was about a young boy who was hanged in Wiesel's concentration camp. Because the child was so small and light, he did not die immediately when the SS tipped over his chair but instead suffered for more than half an hour. "Where is merciful God, where is He?" someone asked who was standing behind Wiesel in the crowd of onlookers. "For God's sake, where is God?" And Wiesel wrote that, from within him, he heard a voice answer: "Where is He? This is where—hanging here from this gallows."[3]

That passage helped me understand that God doesn't stop every panic attack, nor does he stay the finger on the trigger of a barrel pointed in one's own mouth. He doesn't prevent the brain from sloshing into dementia, nor does he protect children from a father who promises to come home early but stays at the bar all night instead. He doesn't stop these things. What he does, I believe, is experience them with us.

He rides out the panic attack, feeling its uncontrolled bursts of adrenaline, and his hands shake as the suicidal person quakes with fear and hatred and utter despair. He comes alongside the disappointed boy, who only wished to see his father for a few moments before bedtime.

He does not take this pain away. What he does is envelope himself in it and whisper:

Me too.

Me too.

Me too.

You cry more during the next week than you have in your entire life. You are thirty-six years old, married, have two beautiful little boys, and you can neither fall asleep at night nor will yourself out of bed in the morning. You fear the light creeping in through the windows, signaling your twelve hours of hiding are coming quickly to an end. You mentally count the number of sleeping pills you have left and wonder if you can spare one for a nap. You have faced depression before, but this—this humiliation and shame—is a completely different animal, and you have no defense for its maniacal onslaught.

You're able to slink from the bed to the playroom to sit with the boys while they watch their morning cartoons. Your wife does everything to get the kids and herself ready for the day. You want to get up and help. You know you should get up and help. You know you need to get up and help. But you don't. You sit and selfishly hold on to those boys because their love for you is unconditional, without judgment, and overflowing with joy. And right now you're hoping that love will be enough to see you through. They both laugh at something Daniel Tiger says on the TV. Will you ever laugh again?

Your wife is a saint. There is no other way to describe it. You have put her in a terrible position, and yet she soldiers on with a strength you know you'll never muster. She is scared. How could she not be? But she doesn't wear her fear for everyone to see like you do. She stands upright, cries in secret, and manages to smile and laugh when she talks to friends and family on the phone. There is a looming problem, but she knows how to deal with problems, overcome problems, and move on from problems. She feels certain, so she says, this problem can be dealt with the same as any other. You, however, are not so sure.

Your doubt is not without proper grounding. The morning after you hit a curb on your way out of the church parking lot, drunk and angry, your boss called and asked, "What can you tell me about last night?"

You explained as best you could, fighting back the pounding in your head. Yes, you'd been drinking. Yes, you've been drinking too much and are aware of it. You'd returned to church for the evening service. It was a big mistake. You are terribly sorry. It will never happen again.

There were follow-up meetings. Questions about your drinking habits. Questions about your prayer life and how much you've been working. There were no specific questions about your mental status; no one inquired as to whether you're feeling depressed or anxious. No one asked whether you're seeing a therapist or plan to. They did, however, ask you to submit to a drug test. They were worried this would offend you. It didn't; you're relieved you're not being fired, and you know the test will come back negative.

In the ensuing days you've been making the necessary apologies to the people who are in the know. You lie to those who aren't. You were sick on the evening of the incident, you say, exhausted and feeling loopy from some unfamiliar medication you took. That is all it was. Nothing else to see here. Can we all please just move on?

So that's what you do.

Move on.

Except you don't.

Because nothing changes, and it's only a matter of time before it all comes crashing down.

FIVE

THIS IS NOT A DRILL

We *all* have a lot of work to do. Most medical professionals agree that we are less than a generation away from turning the corner on cancer. But when it comes to mental health, the car is still parked in the garage. It's a well-accepted embarrassment that twenty years have passed since psychiatry's last major breakthrough treatment for depression. More than fifty years have come and gone since schizophrenia received a meaningful treatment update. Thomas Insel, the former director of the National Institute of Mental Health, summed it up perfectly when he said, "Whatever we've been doing for five decades, it ain't working. . . . When I look at the numbers—the number of suicides, the number of disabilities, the mortality data—it's abysmal, and it's not getting any better. Maybe we just need to rethink this whole approach."[1]

Agreed.

I wish I could say the church has picked up the slack for medicine, but it hasn't. While it's not the church's job to cure mental illness, the church should be a major player in any conversation about caring for those who suffer in their minds. But we haven't been. In fact, in many cases, Christians have been some of the worst offenders when it comes to attaching stigma to mental illness, often attributing it to a spiritual failing, unconfessed sin, flimsy faith, or plain old lack of religious devotion. All of which must absolutely break the heart of Jesus who made it explicitly clear he came not for those who were doing great in life but for those who were sick (Mark 2:17). Jesus embodied the reality that God is always "close to the brokenhearted and saves those who are crushed in spirit" (Ps. 34:18).

And yet when mental illness strikes, it's often the companionship of other Christians we lose first. Given Jesus' propensity to eat and drink with lepers, menstruating women, the paralyzed, the blind—folks the religious people avoided—one might assume the church would wholeheartedly champion the needs of the mentally ill. Instead, only those whose illnesses manifest in traditionally "bodily" forms have been given priority of care.

Break your leg in a snow skiing accident? A church staffer will call you. You might even get a card in the mail. Get diagnosed with breast cancer? The prayer warriors will rally around you and your family. A meal train will get rolling toward your house before you even have a chance to tidy up. Need open heart surgery? Your small group is coming to the hospital. And maybe your pastor too.

But what happens when your wife can't get out of bed to dress your children for school and is eventually diagnosed with major depressive disorder? What about when your twenty-two-year-old son goes missing after a night of smoking weed and is discovered by the police the next day rambling incoherently in a grocery store parking lot and a few weeks later gets diagnosed with schizophrenia?

What does the church do when you're forced to resign your duties as a deacon because you need twenty-eight days to dry out in rehab?

I can tell you what usually happens in these situations. I can tell you what I have seen. The church gets quiet. Like college-library-on-a-Saturday-night quiet. And this silence is not only deafening; it is also spiritually crushing. Because when the church falls down on the job, it feels like God has fallen down on the job—at the worst possible time. Which is something God is really not supposed to do.

Matthew Stanford is a neuroscientist who has studied the relationship between the church and mental illness for decades. Stanford's research has found that local churches in the United States dismiss mental illness at alarmingly high levels. In one study, Stanford polled eighty-five Christians who had been diagnosed with having a mental disorder. More than 40 percent of them reported that someone in their church had suggested they didn't actually have a mental illness.[2]

Can you think of any other form of illness where Christians tell other Christians their doctors don't know what they're talking about? Imagine how foolish a pastor would sound calling you at the hospital to explain your child doesn't actually have cancer. It's ridiculous and would never happen. But when it comes to mental illness, it *does* happen.

A lot.

I manage a Facebook page called Christians and Mental Health. On it I posed the same question Stanford did in his study. I wanted to know if anyone following the page had been diagnosed with a mental disorder by a mental health professional only to be subsequently told by someone in a faith community that the diagnosis wasn't real.[3] The responses flooded my inbox. Below is a sampling of what came back within just a few minutes of posting:

I got told that being on medication would let demons in. This terrified and confused me! I was also told by my pastor that I brought all this upon myself. I eventually wound up in the psychiatric ward of a hospital. It's been nearly four years and I still haven't recovered. Not sure if I ever will.

I have been told over and over again that mental illness is simply the result of a person not spending enough time with God.

I have been diagnosed with multiple mental health conditions. The most common response from my church family is that I hide behind these diagnoses instead of taking responsibility for my actions.

I had postpartum depression after the birth of each of my children. I saw another woman in my church community with the same issues described as "weak" by mutual friends who were in our congregation, and so I kept my diagnosis to myself. I sought help from therapists but not from people in my church. . . . The church does not help with mental health. You'll get lots of sympathy, prayer, and meal trains if you have cancer, but if you're depressed forget it.

A simple question posed to roughly six thousand people. Imagine what we might hear if we keep on asking these kinds of questions? How many other untold stories are out there?

Before I get too preachy about the church dropping the ball and whatnot, I want to acknowledge how tough it is for the church to actually wrap its arms around the mental health of Christians.

A trip to the hospital for a broken leg on a ski trip will probably get broadcast on Facebook because nobody feels shamed by this kind of injury. A photo of you laid up in a hospital bed with a cast wrapped around your swollen leg is likely to garner loads of likes and sympathetic comments. Putting it out there in real time will actually improve your situation as your brain gets dumped with dopamine at all the notifications piling up on your phone. Instead of feeling the pain of your misfortune, you'll be distracted by your instant popularity and its intoxicating effects. Plus, your church will know what happened to you and be able to respond accordingly.

Nobody, however, is photographing themselves lying in their bed at home while experiencing an overwhelming sense of dread at the mere prospect of getting up to take a shower. It's just not happening. And parents, for good reason, are not voluntarily broadcasting the ongoing treatment their newly diagnosed children are receiving for schizophrenia.

All this to say, I understand that the church, in many cases, cannot be expected to respond to situations involving mental illness with the same level of intimate care it so often displays with other types of illnesses and injuries. These aren't perfectly analogous situations. With mental illness there is a lot of secrecy, which can make the task of communal care very, very hard.

But we can do better. We must do better because folks are dying.

And not just a few.

They're dying en masse.

And that's not something Christians can stand by and let happen. It's not something Jesus would stand by and let happen.

MENTAL HEALTH MYTH

MYTH: Mental illness isn't real because it's not mentioned in the Bible.

FALSE. The Bible is an ancient text written for an ancient audience. Consequently, while divinely inspired, its authors only had access to language that was available to them at the time. Given this reality, of course it doesn't specifically mention mental health or mental illness. Just like it doesn't mention Saturn, neurons, or the concept of drag and lift. It's not that these things didn't exist, only that folks were not aware of them in the way that we now are. Nevertheless, the Bible absolutely includes the reality of mental illness in the description of many of its characters.

Do you know what Moses and Job had in common? Both men begged God to kill them (Num. 11:14–15 and Job 3). Even Jesus himself appeared to have had some version of a panic attack in the garden of Gethsemane on the night before his death. "My soul is overwhelmed with sorrow to the point of death" (Matt. 26:38). Those are some gnarly feelings.

Let's also not forget the Bible records about half a dozen suicides.[1]

The strongest argument, however, for the inclusion of mental illness in the Bible is the in-depth treatment of the human psyche offered up in the Psalms. As Steve Bloem said:

The Psalms treat depression more realistically than many of today's popular books on Christianity and psychology. David and other psalmists often found themselves deeply depressed for various reasons. They did not, however, apologize for what they were feeling, nor did they confess it as sin. It was a legitimate part of their relationship with God. They interacted with Him through the context of their depression.[2]

Yes they did. And if the psalmists were free to do it, that means you and I are too.

SIX

ABUNDANT LIFE FOR ALL

I have no interest in throwing unnecessary shade at the church when it comes to how it has traditionally dealt with mental illness. One of the things I love *most* about the church is its fierce commitment to helping those in need. Having worked for nearly a decade in the church as a teacher, lay pastor, and ordained minister, I can attest to the reality that most Christians I've met want to help those in need. Most Christians I know take seriously the command of Jesus to love others as we love ourselves (Mark 12:31). Most Christians I know want to draw more people into the love of God as opposed to leaving them out in the cold. And so I don't think it's some active animus toward those who suffer from mental illness that has kept the church from doing a good job of caring for them. Rather, I think it's been driven mostly by a general confusion about how to actually help.

We don't know what to do, and that's scary. If I'm right, this is good news because we know exactly how to make scary things less scary: we talk about them, openly and honestly. It is human nature to fear what we don't understand. But with understanding usually comes empathy, followed rapidly by harmony.

The church I served in for the better part of a decade hosted an event each summer that I looked forward to all year long called Theology Live. Each Monday night in June we'd gather in a local pub to listen to someone speak on a theological matter for about forty-five minutes before opening the discussion to Q&A from the audience. The idea was to move the conversations we were having in the church to a venue where folks who might never darken the door of a church could participate in them. Each Monday the bar would inevitably fill to capacity and teem with life. It was an electric atmosphere that sometimes made me wish we'd permanently trade our cathedrals and chapels for parks, restaurants, and pubs. But that's a topic for another book entirely.

A few years ago we were planning this event when I suggested we take up the topic of mental health. Judging by the room's reaction you'd have thought I suggested we study the virtues of sex trafficking. The other staffers looked at me as though I'd lost my mind.

"Why would we do that?" someone asked.

"Because it's important," I said. "It affects a lot of people, and the church needs to be talking about it."

"Won't that be fairly depressing?" another person proffered. "Theology Live is serious, I get it, but we want those in attendance to also have a good time. After all, we're in a bar. Do we really want to be talking about suicide or whatever?"

"I don't think anyone *wants* to be talking about suicide," I said, "but I think we *need* to be talking about suicide."

"Nobody will come," someone else said. "It's too uncomfortable."

"I think the opposite will happen," I said.

The debate carried on like this for several weeks. In the end, my idea carried the day, and we did four weeks on mental health.

Guess what?

The bar overflowed with people clamoring to hear from the mental health professionals we invited to discuss the topic. After each talk the comment I heard over and over again from the folks in attendance—often with tears in their eyes—was, "Thank you. Thank you for talking about this."

Families who have been affected by mental illness are dying, in some cases quite literally, for the church to embrace this discussion. But Christians who haven't been directly affected by mental illness are often suspicious of the subject altogether, as my colleagues initially were. For many believers the whole notion of suffering in mind or soul while also trusting Jesus Christ as Lord and Savior is incompatible, or at least very difficult to integrate into their Christian worldview. How *can* one feel as though life isn't worth living while also embracing the love, hope, and forgiveness offered to us by God in Christ Jesus? Shouldn't we simply "count it all joy" as the book of James commands us (1:2 ESV) and get on with our suffering? Sure, life here on earth might be difficult and far from perfect, but that's what heaven is for. While I take these sentiments to be misguided, I do sympathize with those who have them. For a long time I did as well.

Nowhere in the Bible does God promise his followers an easy life. To the contrary, Jesus told his followers to expect trouble in this world (John 16:33). And find trouble they did. Each one of the disciples was executed for his faith, with the exception of John, who was exiled to the island of Patmos, and Judas, who died by suicide. These were the men who literally changed the fate of the world by their willingness to follow Jesus and kick-start the great movement that would eventually become known as Christianity. And they all died. Badly.

And the suffering didn't stop there. Paul, who took up the mantle of the first disciples, boasted of his sufferings for the Lord

(2 Cor. 11:16–33). Consequently, throughout the ages, Christians have often embraced suffering as not only necessary to life but also a sign of living the life God intended for them to live. And, no doubt, this is sometimes the case, as Jesus said it would be when he declared that whoever wanted to become his disciple would need to "deny themselves and take up their cross" and follow him (Mark 8:34).

So, for more than two thousand years, countless Christians have interpreted their own trials and tribulations as forms of taking up their crosses to follow Jesus, enduring whatever life throws their way for the sake of a faith that will be rewarded—perhaps not immediately but certainly eternally. Peace, then, is not to be found in the circumstances of life but in God's peace, which "surpasses all understanding" (Phil. 4:7 ESV).

There is a great deal of wisdom and truth in the line of theological reasoning I've briefly sketched out above. Life is suffering—brutal, unfair, and often very, very cruel and confusing. Just days ago, I read a news story about a young mother who, on Christmas day, threw her two children off the ninth floor of a parking garage before jumping to her own death, leaving behind a husband to mourn the loss of his entire family.[1]

Yes, Jesus told us to expect suffering in this world, sometimes of the unimaginable variety.

But that is not *all* Jesus said.

In fact, in the very same verse where he promised that life will be hard, he also reminded us that he has already overcome this world, a truth he not only articulated with words but also manifested physically in his resurrection from the dead. In life there is suffering and death, but in God there is healing and life. In John's gospel, Jesus said this *life* is the very reason he came to earth. And not just any kind of life but one lived "abundantly" (John 10:10 ESV).

What does that entail?

Well, probably a lot. God's call on our lives is never singular. To live as God intends is to necessarily experience life in all of its diversity. As the book of Ecclesiastes teaches, "There is a time for everything, and a season for every activity under the heavens" (3:1). In other words, yes, the Christian life will necessarily call us to experience hardship and sacrifice, but it should also involve abundance.

But please hear me out on this.

Abundant living is not driving a Range Rover. Sure, Range Rovers are awesome. I don't have anything against Range Rovers. My dad drove a Range Rover when I was in high school, and it was pretty sweet. These days I drive an eleven-year-old dinged-up Volvo. It's not quite as sweet. What *is* sweet, however, is driving that Volvo in abundant peace and with abundant joy.

> For me, abundant living is not about living any version of the high life or succeeding at the American dream—whatever that even means. #millennialprobs
>
> For me, abundant living is not being plagued by panic attacks.
>
> For me, abundant living is not coping with my stress by abusing alcohol.
>
> For me, abundant living is wanting to wake up with the sun instead of hiding out in my bed.
>
> For me, abundant living is doing the things that bring me joy and actually feeling that joy.
>
> For me, abundant living is loving and being loved by God.

That's abundant living, and that's what I believe all of us deserve because Jesus Christ said we do. That includes every person, especially those of us who struggle with our mental health. Abundant living means we also deserve the chance to walk through life not mired forever in the deeper ditches of depression.

Notice I didn't say *depression-free*. A few months ago, a well-meaning friend asked if I was now healed from my depression. I said, "No, I'm not healed, but I am doing much, much better."

The truth is that I'm likely to battle depression and anxiety my entire life because depression is a recurrent disorder. Research indicates that a person who has had one depressive episode has roughly a 60 percent chance of experiencing another one.[2] If the second one does arrive, the chances of having a third grow to 75 percent, and up and up it climbs from there. So, simply put, there are going to be days and nights when I don't feel nearly as good as I do right now, writing this book after having gone for a jog on a sunny Friday morning.

Part of getting real about this disease is accepting the reality that it's often a lifelong disease without, at this point, a known cure. But what often gets forgotten by those of us who struggle is that mental illness—while not curable—is highly treatable. The American Psychiatric Association says that 80 to 90 percent of people with depression experience a noticeable reduction in symptoms if they seek treatment.[3]

Depression and other forms of mental illness are sticky and tend to hang around for a long time. That's reality. What's also reality is that we have a God who inhabits our illnesses and refuses to abandon us to them. What the church needs to do at this moment is get more comfortable declaring this truth in the face of the crippling realities of mental illness.

It's okay that the church cannot eradicate mental illness from the lives of its members. That's nothing to be ashamed about. Those of us who struggle aren't expecting that. What we are expecting, or at the very least hoping for, is that the church won't shy away from our suffering or deny its existence. Please start talking so we can be assured that the promises of Jesus Christ are for us in the same manner they are for everyone else. We need this stated explicitly.

We need talk. Just talk. Nothing more but also nothing less.

We need the kind of talk we got from the artist formerly known as Prince Harry in 2017 when he broke with royal tradition by openly discussing his struggles with mental health. As you likely know, Harry and his brother, William, lost their mother, Princess Diana, in a tragic car accident when they were both young boys. Harry said he spent his teenage years and twentysomethings dodging thoughts of his mother's death. "My way of dealing with it was sticking my head in the sand, refusing to ever think about my mum, because why would that help? I thought it's only going to make you sad, it's not going to bring her back."[4] In the mid-2000s, Harry joined the British Army around the same time his drunken antics invited ruthless media attention.

Despite these few PR snafus, Harry rose to the rank of an Apache helicopter commander and served valiantly in battle. His military success, however, opened the door for speculation that his mental health challenges were related to his time at war, a notion Harry vehemently rebuffed. "I can safely say it's not Afghanistan-related. . . . I'm not one of those guys that has had to see my best mate blown up next to me. . . . Thank God, I wasn't one of those people."[5]

It was the way Harry had been forced to publicly grieve—and as a result hardly grieve at all—that did the most damage to his psyche. He said he didn't let his "emotions be part of anything."[6] But then he had a few honest conversations with trusted family and friends and realized he had some serious issues that needed to be worked through. So that's what he did. He got honest with himself and dealt with the trauma buried deep in his past.

Here's where this story gets interesting for me and I hope for you as well. Harry said it was his brother, Prince William, who encouraged him to seek help from a mental health professional. Think about the significance of that. There are millions, if not billions, of people around the world who believe going to therapy is something to be ashamed of because it represents some sort of failure in life, be it moral, spiritual, or otherwise. But here is the future king of England, the head of "one of the most buttoned-up, traditional institutions on the planet,"[7] encouraging his brother to seek help and then be honest about it with the *entire world*.

That, my friends, is what you call the turning of a page in history. If the royal family isn't ashamed of addressing mental health, then the church can't be either. A journalist, reflecting on her time with Prince Harry, said, "It has always been a sign of strength and dignity to keep it all inside, and our Royal family have always been the embodiment of that, God bless them. But Prince Harry [with his honesty] just redefined strength and dignity for a new generation."[8]

Reminds me of what another guy said a long time ago writing to the church in Corinth about the time he was taken up in glory to see the Lord. To keep Paul from becoming conceited about this experience, the Lord placed *a thorn in his flesh to torment him* (2 Cor. 12:7, emphasis added). Paul begged the Lord to take it away but, alas, to no avail. We have no idea, of course, what that thorn actually was, only that it helped Paul understand that, no matter what he achieved in life or what privileges he was granted, he was nothing apart from God. When Paul asked God to take the thorn away, God replied, "My grace is sufficient for you, for my power is made perfect in weakness" (v. 9), leading Paul to boldly declare, "For when I am weak, then I am strong" (v. 10).

The abundant life is not about living without pain or having all the answers or all the cures. It is about trusting that the life of Jesus Christ and his great provisions will be enough for us to not simply survive but thrive.

The church is in a unique position to spread this message far and wide. It need only do what Prince William did for Prince Harry: encourage those who suffer to seek the help they need from the professionals who have the expertise to provide it, then boldly declare that what was true for Paul is still true for all of us today.

God's power is made perfect in weakness.

SEVEN

EPIDEMIC

I only got honest about my depression and anxiety because I had no other choice. For years I suspected that I needed to speak to a professional, but I only did so once the pain became too much for me to handle on my own. In other words, I went in there kicking and screaming. I always marvel at my clients who show up in my office at the first sign of trouble, these folks who seem keenly aware of how important it is to acknowledge their pain and be honest about their feelings. It took me forever to learn the value of that lesson. I hope to one day become more like my brave clients. I *am* a therapist, and sometimes I still struggle to make the appointment.

It was the blasted panic attacks that finally wore me down. If you've never had a panic attack, congratulations, you have won some version of the genetic lottery. These bad boys are chemical hurricanes in the brain that convince you you're about to die, and they do not listen to reason or weighted blankets or even the best Taylor Swift song of all time. And that's saying something because I love me some Taylor Swift and a well-designed weighted blanket. Short of sedation, though, there is nothing that can be done during a panic attack other than to ride it out and repeatedly tell yourself that you're not going to die while trying like mad to believe it.

For me, they'd creep up at night just as I was trying to fall asleep. One moment I'd be lying peacefully in bed. The next, my heart would begin to race and sweat would break out across my back. Not long after, my mind would feel scrambled, and I'd be thrown back into some kind of twisted nightmare from childhood where I'm convinced the dark will never give way to the light.

This will pass, I'd tell myself. I'd try and take a deep breath but then realize I couldn't take a deep breath, which only served to crank up the anxiety further. Death was imminent.

Maybe getting out of bed would help? Maybe drinking some water or walking up and down the stairs a few times would dispel the miserable feeling? I mean, where had it even come from in the first place? How dare my mind betray me while in my own bed at night!

I'd drink the water. I'd do the steps. But the storm would still rage. Any attempt to beat back the waves proved futile. I'd settle for sinking into the fetal position beside my bed, vacillating between prayers of petition and anger to God, all while feeling humiliated for looking like this in front of my wife, who expected and needed me to be strong. I had responsibilities. I had an infant sleeping in the next room. I didn't have time for this. I didn't ask for this.

All feelings mental illness doesn't care about.

It's like you're drowning in your own thoughts. Your brain convinces your mind that it's all over and there is nothing you can do to combat it. Helpless doesn't even get close to the impotence you feel in this moment. It's as though the very cells of your body declare mutiny and attack you all at once. There is seemingly no way to defend against the enemy that comes from within. It doesn't matter if you're a lifelong Christian or a worship leader or a pastor, like me, because Christians are not exempt. Not by a long shot.

I wish that being a Christian protected us from mental illness. I wish that opening our lives to the power of the Holy Spirit provided a safeguard from depression and anxiety and bipolar disorder and any of the other disorders and diseases that mess with our brains and emotional well-being. I wish so badly that I could tell a person contemplating suicide that the love of God would dissipate this desire. I wish so badly that telling a woman who has been raped by her biological father that her heavenly Father never wanted the abuse to happen would make her trauma easier to process. I wish I could tell a person addicted to opioids that freedom in Christ is the greatest high in the world. I wish that all of these truths—and they are truths—were enough to carry a person from sickness to health. But they're not.

When it comes to mental illness, like all suffering, our faith makes no promise of exemption. I can't find any promise in Scripture that Jesus will alleviate our suffering or even offer a clear explanation for what is taking place. What I do find on those ancient pages is a Jesus who attends deeply and cares mightily and is willing to sit in each and every instance of pain he encounters. Because he was fully human, he understood that human pain is universally complicated and no amount of Christian maturity allows a person to opt out of the intractable ways our brains and souls work well and not so well together.

Charles Spurgeon is widely considered to have been one of the greatest preachers who ever lived. He also suffered from debilitating bouts of depression. Mr. Spurgeon experienced the dizzying heights of God's love while also wallowing in the seemingly bottomless pits of an afflicted mind. And yet God still used him for glorious purposes. The same went for the English poet William Cowper, who lost his mother at age six and battled suicidal thoughts for decades. Amidst the throes of sorrow and suffering, he and his pastor-friend John Newton managed to compose the hymn "Amazing Grace." Not too shabby. What I mean to say is that Christian faith, while enormously helpful in fighting mental illness, does not provide immunity from it.

Why not?

Because our souls, like our bodies, are affected by the fallen nature of this world. That is to say, our souls do not get a pass on suffering.

Nobody gets a hall pass from the consequences outlined in Genesis 3,[1] when God's good creation got dinged by Adam and Eve's decision to do life on their own terms. And when I say nobody, I mean nobody, not even the GOAT himself.[2]

In the garden of Gethsemane, on the night before his crucifixion, Jesus said this to his disciples, "My soul is overwhelmed with sorrow to the point of death. Stay here and keep watch with me" (Matt. 26:38). If the soul of Jesus ran into trouble in this life, surely we can expect ours will as well. Jesus told his friends he felt so overwhelmed he might die right there on the spot. If you've ever had a panic attack, you know the man wasn't exaggerating. The tightening

---

1 If you're not totally boned up on Christian theology, no worries, I got your back. The basic idea is that God's intention for humanity was for us to live in the full presence of his goodness, but we chose instead to rebel against his plan because we thought we knew better. Consequently, humans live in a state of perpetual tension we call sin. This sin, in a very real way, separates us from God. In short, life as it currently stands with all its pain and suffering is not what God intended life to be. And it's our fault. The sin of Adam and Eve is not something that happened once but happens every day when we choose to live apart from God's all-inclusive love. The good news, however, is that through the life, death, and resurrection of Jesus, we have been given a way back to the good life in God. More on all of this later. In short: the world is messed up. Shocker, I know.

2 GOAT means "greatest of all time."

of the chest. The inability to catch a deep breath. The tingling sensation running down your arms. Your brain's wild cacophony of alarms screeching that *this is the end*. That's most likely what Jesus was experiencing. He wasn't simply nervous or stressed out by the prospect of getting nailed to a tree. He was suffering in the extreme. He was, to put it bluntly, having a mental health episode because, *yes*, he was *that* human.

Some of you are unsettled about what I just wrote. If you are, take a deep breath while I try and explain. I'm not saying Jesus lost his mind or was mentally ill. What I am saying is that he freaked out righteously in that garden. *"My soul is overwhelmed with sorrow to the point of death."* Modern translation: "Yo, guys, I think I'm dying over here!"

No soul is immune from sickness. Like the brain, the soul is powerful but subject to illness. When this happens, it needs repair. When either the brain or the soul falls ill, the results often manifest as mental illness. If not treated properly, the consequences can be ruinous. Despite what many in the church have said through the ages, this can even happen to individuals of tremendous faith. After all, I think it happened to Jesus.

It definitely happened to Jarrid Wilson, a prominent pastor who, on September 9, 2019, hopped on Twitter and wrote:

> Loving Jesus doesn't always cure suicidal thoughts.
>
> Loving Jesus doesn't always cure depression.
>
> Loving Jesus doesn't always cure PTSD.
>
> Loving Jesus doesn't always cure anxiety.
>
> But that doesn't mean Jesus doesn't offer us companionship
> and comfort.
>
> He *always* does that.[1]

Jarrid was right.

At no point in the Bible does God offer us protection from suffering. But we are told that God will never abandon us to our troubles. I think *that* was the point Jarrid was making.

There is a good reason we Christians put a cross at the center of our religion. We serve a God who does not always remove suffering but always understands suffering and chooses to suffer with us. That's what the cross represents: the deep love and affection God has for people.

Before Jarrid tweeted the post I mentioned above, he had already tweeted that he'd be "officiating a funeral for a Jesus-loving woman who took her own life." He then asked for prayers for the family of the deceased.[2] Later that day, Jarrid performed his pastoral duties at the funeral. By all accounts, he did so with grace and professionalism.

And then, that night, on the eve of World Suicide Prevention Day, Jarrid completed suicide.

I'm sorry, but I have to pause here and take a big breath. For real. Feel free to use the next page, which I left blank, as an invitation to stop reading and do the same. We can't blow past any person's suicide, not if we're going to make any headway in slowing these deaths down. Take a moment. Be wounded by Jarrid's wounding. Weep for Jarrid. Weep for his family. Weep for someone you've lost to suicide. If you're feeling really brave, write that person's name down in the blank space as a permanent reminder for why you're reading this book. It's completely fine if it's your own name you need to put there.

Jarrid's death stunned a lot of people, myself included. Just a few weeks before his death, we had connected online because a particular Instagram post of his had lifted my soul on a day when I felt cruddy. I was so moved by it that I actually read it aloud to my wife as we crawled into bed one evening. Jarrid wrote, "I'm a Christian who also struggles with depression. This exists, and it's okay to admit it."[3]

Because of Jarrid's honesty and bravery, I fell asleep that night feeling a little less alone with my pain. Here was a guy who, by all accounts, was beloved for all the righteous reasons. He was a loving husband and father, a devoted pastor, an accomplished author, and a man brave enough to openly discuss his struggles with mental health. To me, Jarrid was a shining example of what Christians ought to be: authentic, humble, and hopeful.

And yet we lost him. Just like we continue to lose so many others.

In 2017, more than 47,000 people completed suicide in the United States.[4] If you're doing the math, that means we lose someone about every eleven minutes. When you consider the global population, the time frame shrinks down to forty seconds. Think about that. Someone in this beautiful world of ours takes their own life every forty seconds. That amounts, globally, to around 800,000 people.[5] That's all the folks in San Francisco gone. Poof. Just like that.

Let. It. Spin. Your. Head.

It's unacceptable, especially when you consider these numbers are undoubtedly unreported because families often do not want suicides officially documented by authorities. Moreover, deaths from the opioid crisis (about 70,000 a year) are not included in the figure above.[6]

It's bad, y'all. This whole situation is a massive fire that, if not put out, will burn a brand of destruction our society has never seen.

I'm ringing the bell. This is not a drill. There is no time to wait.

News of Jarrid's death broke on Tuesday, September 10, World Suicide Prevention Day. Just before I learned of his death, two things happened that I want to tell you about.

First, my literary agent, Amanda, called to tell me the book you're reading would be published. As a writer you're never quite sure which, if any, of your projects will actually make it to publication. Talk to any serious writer, and you're likely to discover that person has multiple completed manuscripts that will never see the light of day. I wrote for almost ten years before being published. Publication is a big deal for us writers. This offer was especially big because I'm so passionate about this particular topic. Destigmatizing mental illness in the Christian community is one of the primary calls God has placed upon my life. Consequently, when Amanda called, my instinct was to close my laptop and speed home to tell my wife the good news. But it was World Suicide Prevention Day, and I'd been writing a Facebook post about it when she called. I needed to finish that post before going home to celebrate. So that's what I did.

This was my post:

On October 29 of last year, Lion Air Flight 610 took off in Indonesia at 6:20 a.m. local time. Twelve minutes later, the plane crashed into the Java Sea, killing all 189 passengers and crew. Nearly five months later, Ethiopian Airlines Flight 302 took off from Ethiopia at 8:38 a.m. local time. Six minutes later, that plane also crashed, killing all 157 people aboard. Both jets were Boeing 737 Max 8s, a variant of the bestselling aircraft in history.

On March 12, two days after the second 737 Max went down, I took a 737 Max 8 from Dallas to Los Angeles. I was scheduled to fly home on another 737 Max 8 on March 14. Before I could fly home, President Trump grounded the aircraft in the US, a move that caused myself and millions of other people to be delayed. It was annoying, sure, but it was necessary to ensure our safety.

Think about this with me. Two planes go down. Three hundred and forty-six people die. And because we're uncertain why, our government takes an extreme measure to ensure it doesn't happen again.

In the US alone, more than 47,000 people died by suicide in 2017. Globally, someone completes suicide every forty seconds. It's an epidemic. And the most recent studies suggest it's only getting worse.

Last night I went to a support group for lawyers who battle depression. I really like this particular group because the level of honesty in there is remarkable. For some of these folks, suicide is a constant option in their lives. It haunts them, taunts them, and oftentimes begs them to just get on with it and out of life.

As I listened to friends share ways they've prevented themselves from killing themselves, I couldn't help but think: *This is the very essence of soul care. These people are actually willing to stare into the darkest recesses of their souls, do battle with what they find there, and then emerge wounded but alive. These are people who know that Saint John was right when he wrote, "There is a light shining in the darkness and the darkness has not overcome it"* [paraphrase of John 1:5].

Today is World Suicide Prevention Day, and I want to honor every person who's ever battled suicide ideation, survived an attempt, or continues to love someone who completed suicide. Please know there are so many of us who honor you and will take whatever extreme measure is needed to reduce these numbers. There's no magic pill, but there are practical solutions and very smart and compassionate people working their hardest to come up with more.

We won't stop fighting. So you don't either.[7]

Moments after I published the post, I scrolled down and saw a post from my good friend Rashawn Copeland saying that Jarrid was gone. The excitement I'd felt moments earlier instantly vanished. It was one of those moments when the world slows down and you can't trust the information your brain is feeding you. I *had* to be reading the post incorrectly. I read Rashawn's post again. Then I read it again. One more time.

Oh, man. I *was* reading it correctly. Jarrid was gone. The pastor who had lifted my spirit only *days* before had now taken his own life. I closed my laptop and drove home in silence. There would be no celebration that evening. I had work to do.

EIGHT

THE PROBLEM OF SUICIDE

My first brush with suicide came in the seventh grade when I learned that my camp counselor from the previous summer, a college student I idolized, had gone to a park where my older brother and I regularly went rollerblading and shot himself in the head with a shotgun.

The mechanics of the affair initially dominated my mind. How, exactly, does a person get a shotgun into their mouth? "With their toe," my brother informed me. The image still haunts me. You have to take off your shoe. You must carefully put the gun in place. And then you must find the trigger with your toe and carefully bend it around the trigger, knowing it'll be the last thing you ever do. Do you hear the blast from the shot? Are you scared in the millisecond before it happens? Is there pain, or do you simply vanish in the bang? I didn't know, and I could not stop thinking about it.

The other thing I couldn't stop thinking about was everything my counselor had done and said during our time together. He was funny. He told me about Jesus. He got me really excited about going to college someday. He was as full of life as any person I have ever known. I was utterly dumbfounded that he would die this way. But that was only because I knew nothing about depression. I didn't know that depression can invade a person's mind and stay there without permission. I didn't know that depression is a liar and a thief who sets out to plunder and destroy.

Looking back, I hope someone talked to me about depression in the wake of his death, but I honestly can't remember that happening. All I remember the adults telling us was that sometimes people do this to themselves.

That really freaked me out, especially because this suicide was the first of many that would follow.

The father of my mother's best friend.

The father of my brother's high school sweetheart.

The brother of a good friend.

The quiet kid who lived down the street.

On and on it went throughout the years, each death growing scarier in my mind than the last one as I realized suicide didn't discriminate. The reality that someone I loved might die at their own hand sent shivers down my spine.

It still does.

A friend and I were recently talking about his own depressive episode, which was the first of his life. He was just learning to swim in its deep waters but doing a heck of a job at it. He asked me if I had ever been suicidal, and I almost lied to him. I wanted to tell him, no, I have never had this dark thought, that I don't get *that* depressed. But the truth is that I've been far closer to it than I'd like to admit. The truth is that, in one particularly bad moment, I hysterically told my wife that I understood why people killed themselves before running out of the room and into my closet where I sobbed uncontrollably.

I was in a deep depression at the time, and it felt as if my pain would never end. I didn't want to die, but I desperately needed the pain to stop. I found this incredibly shameful to admit to my friend, which I eventually did. I find it even more shameful to write this to you because it recently happened again while I was writing this book. I dread the day my children read these words. But it happened. I did have the dark thought. Twice. I said the dark words. Twice. And so there it is. When I get honest with myself, I know that madness is not a stranger living in a foreign land but a familiar knocking at my door that I sometimes must work hard not to answer.

After Jarrid's death, several friends asked me how this sort of thing could happen. How does a young, successful pastor with a gorgeous family die by suicide? It's all very confusing.

I wasn't suicidal in the summer of 2018 when I tried to preach drunk, but let me tell you something: I was in a whole lot of pain. Pain that was so intense it did have me considering my options. Something far more of us do than we realize. In fact, more than nine million Americans seriously consider it each year.[1] Just the other night, I watched Billie Eilish become the first woman in the history of the GRAMMY Awards to take home album of the year, record of the year, song of the year, and be named best new artist. Before the awards show aired, Eilish told Gayle King in an interview that she had experienced some very dark days while touring in 2018. She said, "I was so unhappy, and I was so, like, joyless. I don't want to be too dark, but I genuinely didn't think I'd make it to 17."[2] When asked a follow-up question, Eilish confirmed that she'd had suicidal thoughts.

These sorts of thoughts come and go in far more people than we realize. Suicide is scary, which is why we have to talk about it more openly and honestly. I believe the more we speak out about how many people struggle with these thoughts, the more we will help reduce the number of people who follow through with these thoughts. So in an effort to do just that, I'm going to address some of the more common questions I hear about suicide in hopes that it might not only be practically helpful for those who are curious but also work as a reminder that we cannot have a genuinely honest conversation about mental health unless we also talk about its most extreme form of damage: suicide.

NOBODY REALLY WANTS TO DIE, RIGHT?

Hardwired into human beings is a longing to stay alive for as long as we possibly can. Even before a child learns of death, that child acts in self-preserving ways, breathing and eating and recoiling from danger. When the concept of death does arrive, the fear of it usually follows shortly thereafter. My wife and I are currently in the thick of raising two young boys, and they sometimes ask us about death, wondering what happens to people when they die, if it hurts, and whether or not children can also die. We try to be as honest with them as we can.

What happens? I don't know exactly, but I trust that when we die we do so into the safety and everlasting love of God.

Does it hurt? Sometimes, but not always. Sometimes death is a relief for a person who is very old or very ill. It is the natural order of things for life to run its course and end.

Can children die? It's less common, but yes, children can and do die, but it's always very sad when they do. Always.

During these conversations with our boys, who are the epitome of rowdy, they display a raw tenderness that tells me they understand death is a sacred topic. Instinctively, they know that what we are talking about is mysterious, a bit scary, but also profoundly important. They somehow know that learning about death is a worthwhile thing to do because life is precious and deserving of tremendous care and protection. Living is good.

When mental illness is severe enough, however, living feels far less good and death not nearly as scary. Instead of hoping to avoid death, it becomes an attractive exit from pain. Simone Biles, the Olympic champion gymnast, suffers from depression and has said that when she is depressed she sleeps as much as she can because sleep is "the closest thing to death" she can find.[3] I do the exact same thing. It's why I have abused Ambien. I can take a pill, and the lights go out. Instant relief.

If you haven't been depressed, this can be hard to understand. To better empathize, try to think of a time when you experienced the worst physical pain of your life. Maybe it was childbirth or a broken bone or a long recovery from a complicated surgery. In the moments of your most intense suffering, what would you have done to simply get the pain to stop? Just about anything, right? Now imagine the pain isn't in your leg but manifesting in your very thoughts, from which you cannot escape. Unconsciousness can become the only way we who suffer from depression find relief. The trouble with sleep is that you inevitably have to wake up. In death, however, the sleep never ends. And so, for the suicidal person, suicide is not so much about ending life as it is about ending pain. Do they want to live? Probably. But can they continue living in so much pain? Probably not.

IS SUICIDE A SIN?

For centuries the Roman Catholic Church's position on suicide was so severe the church would not even bury a person who died by suicide in ground it considered to be holy. Fortunately, the church has softened its position, both in doctrine and in practice. Thanks to Pope John Paul II, the current *Catechism of the Catholic Church* acknowledges the reality that mental illness "can diminish the responsibility of the one committing suicide." That said, the *Catechism* also states, "We are obliged to accept life gratefully and preserve it for [God's] honor and the salvation of our souls. We are stewards, not owners, of the life God has entrusted to us. It is not ours to dispose of."[4] While this is a teaching specific to Catholicism, I think most Christians would agree with the statement, given that the Bible says, "Do you not know that . . . you are not your own? For you were bought at a price; therefore glorify God in your body" (1 Cor. 6:19–20 NKJV).

Our lives are gifts that we possess but only in part. We dwell in our bodies along with God himself. In the same passage cited above, Paul explicitly said that a human body "is the temple of the Holy Spirit." Given this reality, suicide can appear an unthinkable act for a Christian because it's not only a rejection of the gift of life but also a desecration of a holy place where God has chosen to dwell. Consequently, the vast majority of Christian tradition has cast suicide as not only a sin but a grave one at that. Saint Augustine reasoned it was sinful because it obviously violated the sixth commandment, "You shall not murder" (Ex. 20:13; Deut. 5:17). Henceforth, there has been little departure from this line of thinking. G. K. Chesterton laid out this position rather succinctly, if not brutally:

> Not only is suicide a sin, it is the sin. It is the ultimate and absolute evil, the refusal to take an interest in existence; the refusal to take the oath of loyalty to life. The man who kills a man, kills a man. The man who kills himself, kills all men; as far as he is concerned he wipes out the whole world.[5]

I greatly admire Chesterton, but his take on suicide is just plain wrong. Suicide takes the life of one person but not necessarily of those who are left behind. Yes, suicide greatly affects the grieving process in ways that other deaths do not. No doubt about it. In fact, recovering from the death of a loved one's suicide is as close to an impossible task as any on earth. That said, I have seen the miracle of resurrection in the lives of my friends and clients who not only rise from these ashes but also find ways to grow into more beautiful creatures than they were before the suicide. Suicide inflicts pain on all people, but it doesn't kill all people. Some people, like my friend Terry, are born anew in its wake.

Terry watched her first husband violently take his life in front of her, leaving her alone to raise their four daughters. Years later, Terry's youngest daughter also died by suicide. I think it's safe to say most people would wilt under that kind of suffering. But that's not what Terry did. Terry carried on, loving her daughters fiercely and becoming one of the most effective suicide prevention advocates in the country, tirelessly spreading a message of hope and resilience to anyone and everyone who needs it. Suicide is the worst, but it doesn't bring out the worst in everyone—some people, people like Terry, take the disaster and turn it into something gorgeous and healing for the good of other people. The Bible says that God can make all things work for good (Rom. 8:28). Folks like Terry are living proof of that.

Furthermore, casting all suicide as sinful fails to seriously account for the reality that many suicides are not acts of volition but the inevitable consequence of mental illness. Roughly 90 percent of people who die by suicide suffer from some form of a psychiatric disorder at the moment of death.[6] And it's not just mental illness that places a person at increased risk for suicide but also, according to the National Institute of Mental Health, certain medical conditions, chronic pain, abuse of drugs or alcohol, prior suicide attempts, a family history of suicide, abuse, and exposure to other suicides—to name but a few of the complicating factors.[7] In other words, suicide, like mental illness itself, is hardly ever the result of a singular cause but rather comes about from a confluence of factors, many of which are beyond the control of the person who dies. All of which leads me to conceive of suicide not so much as a sin but yet another tragic consequence of our shared original sin. We live in an unfathomably broken and fallen world. And in that world, some people have no choice but to hand back to God the very thing they ought to cherish most. I'm not saying it's right or that it's good, only that it is.

But even if suicide is a sin (and maybe sometimes it is), it should never be described as unforgivable, as has often been the case in Christianity. For who among us has the right to stand in God's place of judgment? It is God who forgives sin and no one else. Furthermore, it is God's right to choose whom and when he forgives. To claim that any soul—in this life or in the next—lies somehow beyond the mercy of God is simply not a position I'm comfortable taking.

What I do take great comfort in, however, are the words of Paul in Romans 8, with whom I'll give the final word on this question of suicide as sin:

And I am convinced that nothing can ever separate us from God's love. Neither death nor life, neither angels nor demons, neither our fears for today nor our worries about tomorrow— not even the powers of hell can separate us from God's love. No power in the sky above or in the earth below—indeed, nothing in all creation will ever be able to separate us from the love of God that is revealed in Christ Jesus our Lord.

WHAT SHOULD I BE ON THE LOOKOUT FOR IF I'M WORRIED ABOUT SOMEONE'S MENTAL HEALTH?

While there are certain indicators that a person is suicidal, there is no definitive method for accurately predicting who will make an attempt and who will not. Suicides are much like the tornados that sometimes sweep across my home state of Texas: unpredictable. The best meteorologists can do is alert us when conditions are ripe for a tornado so we can be prepared to take cover in the event one actually touches down. Similarly, we can't predict a suicide, but we can be on the lookout for certain signs that indicate one might be brewing:

- Changes in a person's *personality* (A friend who is normally the life of the party might suddenly become much quieter in social settings and begin to skip out on social events altogether. Likewise, a more reserved or naturally sullen person might begin displaying extremely extroverted behavior. Someone who never drinks might suddenly begin binge drinking and engaging in other risky behavior.)
- Changes in a person's typical *behavior* (A friend might begin complaining about a once-loved job as if it's nothing but a burden. The person might also lose focus and begin underperforming at work or stop going to work altogether.)
- Changes in a person's day-to-day *attitude* (A friend who is the eternal optimist might start suddenly talking about how

nothing is ever going to get better, seeing things in a negative light, and complaining about everything.)

In short, if a loved one who has been depressed makes any sudden and dramatic changes in personality, behavior, or attitude, it's worth having a conversation about what's going on.

WHAT CAN I DO TO HELP?

Observing the warning signs for suicide is one thing, but then doing something about it is an entirely different matter. Below I have sketched out four things that all of us can do for the people in our lives for whom we are concerned. None of these things are difficult in nature, nor do they require any specific set of training or skills. The thing they do demand, however, is courage.

Ask. Ask. Ask.

Don't settle for asking the person you're worried about, "Are you feeling okay?" Ask, "Are you suicidal?" Be blunt. There is no downside to asking. You will not plant the idea or make the person more likely to attempt suicide. All of that is nonsense. What asking does is make the person feel acknowledged, which is likely a reminder that people care. You will never regret asking someone about suicide. What you will regret, undoubtedly, is not asking. When in doubt, just ask.

On September 25, 2000, a young man named Kevin Hines stood on the Golden Gate Bridge and looked down at the water 220 feet below him. A voice inside his head implored him to jump off. If he jumped, he would most certainly die. Since the bridge opened in

1937, it is estimated that more than 1,700 people have used it to end their lives. Only twenty-five are known to have survived the fall. Kevin did not expect to become the twenty-sixth.

On the day Kevin traveled to the bridge to consider jumping, he made a pact with himself. If just one person, any person, approached him and asked if he was okay, then he wouldn't jump. That was the deal. All he needed to know was that there was at least one person in the world willing to inquire about his well-being. It didn't have to be a family member or a friend—a perfect stranger would have done the trick. But the perfect strangers who rode the bus with Kevin while he openly wept chose to stare and point at him instead of asking if he needed help.

When he got to the bridge, he still held out hope. A few smiling tourists approached him but only to ask if he would take their picture. The voice in his head grew louder, imploring him to jump.

So this nineteen-year-old kid fighting hard through mental illness and the trauma of his parents' divorce got a running start and leapt over the railing, plunging headfirst toward the water.

Miraculously, Kevin *did* become that unexpected twenty-sixth survivor. He now spends his days telling his story and offering hope to untold numbers of people battling mental illness.

Never, never underestimate the power of *the ask*. You just might save a person's life.

Listen. Listen. Listen.

You don't have to know what to say to help a suicidal person. In many cases, you won't need to say much of anything at all. The simple act of listening and providing your physical presence can be quite helpful. The most important thing is to refrain from opining on the situation by making judgments about the hurting person's life or feelings. There is no need to try and offer answers to questions you don't know the answer to. You can always fall back on recommending the person go and speak to a professional for guidance. It's okay to say, "I don't know, but I bet a therapist or doctor would. You should call one and ask."

You are that person's loved one, and that is all you need to be. As the Bible says, "Above all, love each other deeply, because love covers over a multitude of sins" (1 Peter 4:8). Don't keep from asking because you are afraid you'll say something wrong. When in doubt, just be quiet and listen. But if you feel like you must say something, you can't go wrong with any of the following:

- You are important in my life.
- I am so glad you are here.
- I can't begin to imagine what you are going through, but I am here for you.
- You matter.
- If you want to talk to me about how you're feeling, I promise to listen. I don't care how long it takes.
- If you don't want to talk, I'm happy to sit here in silence if you'd like me to. I just enjoy spending time with you.
- You have never been a burden to me.
- You are not a burden to me now.
- I don't understand how feelings work, but I know mine always seem to be changing.
- It sounds like you feel hopeless. Would you mind if I carried hope for you for a while?

For the moments when you don't feel like you have anything to say, remember the words of Henri Nouwen: "The friend who can be silent with us in a moment of despair or confusion, who can stay with us . . . who can tolerate not-knowing, not-curing, not-healing and face with us the reality of our powerlessness, that is the friend who cares."[8]

Keep at it.

Don't settle for a single conversation. Bringing up suicide for the first time with a depressed person can feel awkward. Doing it a second and third time can be even more awkward because it feels intrusive. But it's not like you're asking someone on a date who has already turned you down. You're trying to save the life of a friend. It is incumbent on those of us who are concerned about someone to be persistent in our efforts.

The suicidal person is often in a fluid situation that can change day by day and even moment by moment. Just because someone wasn't suicidal yesterday does not mean the same is true today. If you believe a loved one is suicidal, you should check on that person every single day. Does that feel extreme? Good. It is. Feeling suicidal is an extreme situation that requires extreme assistance.

Watch the news.

High-profile suicides of people like Anthony Bourdain or Kate Spade or televisions shows like *13 Reasons Why* that receive a great deal of attention in the media can put an already at-risk person at further risk of suicide. In the month following the debut of *13 Reasons Why*, there was a 28.9 percent increase in suicide among Americans ages ten to seventeen. This spike represented the largest researchers had seen when studying a five-year period. Over the rest of that year, there were 195 more youth suicides than historical trends would have suggested.[9] When any suicide-themed show or news story trends on social media, it's especially important to reach out to loved ones and see how they're doing.

HOW DO I SURVIVE THE AFTERMATH OF A SUICIDE?

Surviving the suicide of a loved one must be one of the more difficult and heroic things any person can do. Grieving any death is difficult, but suicide is particularly hard because a suicide creates questions that other deaths do not. Most notably, those who lose a loved one in this way wonder what they could have done differently or whether they are to share in the responsibility of the death itself.

I have never spoken to a suicide survivor who has not struggled with the idea that they somehow contributed to the suicide of their loved one. Many describe nights of endless rumination. If they could only go back in time and say *this* instead of *that*. If only they had taken the warning signs more seriously. If only they had asked more questions. If only they had been more sensitive. If only they had been a better parent or spouse or friend.

If only.

If only.

If only.

The truth is that suicide is almost never brought about by one factor. Most likely you did everything you could for your loved one. Did you make mistakes? Of course. Nobody loves anyone perfectly. That's why we have Jesus. If you find yourself ruminating over what you could have done differently to somehow prevent the suicide, I need you to do two things for me:

1. Go see a therapist to process your grief and guilt.
2. Make this your mantra: *It's not my fault.*

ONE FINAL THOUGHT

Earlier in the book I said that our souls and our bodies can become sick with mental illness. It is not simply a disorder of the brain but can also be one of the soul. What is important to note from a Christian perspective is that, while mental illness has the power to injure the soul, it cannot kill our souls.

Jesus said, "Do not fear those who kill the body but cannot kill the soul. Rather fear him who can destroy both soul and body in hell" (Matt. 10:28 ESV).

God alone holds the power to truly extinguish a life. All we humans can do is stop a body from living. The life within cannot be snuffed out, not by any amount of illness or violence.

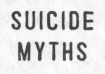

SUICIDE MYTHS

MYTH: People who talk about suicide aren't the ones who actually do it.

FACT: Two-thirds of people who die by suicide talk about their intentions beforehand.[1] Even if not in explicit terms, they might talk about life as "not worth living" or the fact that they "won't be around too much longer." Consequently, it's critical to take any mention of suicide seriously. Never assume someone who is talking about suicide is merely doing so as a way of gaining attention.

MYTH: Only the truly mentally ill consider suicide.

FACT: One in five college students will consider suicide in a twelve-month time period.[2]

MYTH: Suicide cannot be prevented once a person decides to make an attempt.

FACT: Feeling suicidal is almost always a temporary feeling. Those who study suicide have found that most suicidal people are far more ambivalent about dying than determined to do so, thus highlighting the importance of helping the suicidal person receive proper treatment. Research shows that suicide attempts are up to thirty times more common than completed suicides, indicating that the suicidal person often has very mixed emotions about the act. It's almost always a mistake to assume nothing can be done for the suicidal person. Until a suicide is completed, it remains the most preventable of all deaths.

MYTH: Talking about suicide is dangerous because it highlights the option for someone who is already considering it.

FACT: This is like saying we shouldn't talk to teenagers about sex because it might plant the idea in their heads. Too late. They're teenagers, which means they're thinking about sex. The same goes for the truly depressed when it comes to suicide. Even if not actively suicidal, the idea has most likely already entered their minds. Most people who are suicidal are desperate to have someone to talk to about their thoughts, feelings, and life circumstances. Bringing up the topic is far more likely to save a life than take one.

MYTH: Once suicidal, always suicidal.

FACT: Thousands of individuals who seriously contemplate or even go so far as to attempt suicide recover and go on to live healthy, happy, and productive lives.

NINE

WHO ARE WE?

Around the time I got in trouble at church I was unwell. I was exhausted—physically, emotionally, relationally, and spiritually. You might say I had not been paying proper attention to the complexity of my biopsychosocial makeup. I was completely burned out and suffering major compassion fatigue. I remember an elderly couple weeping in my office about the fact that their gay son had told them he never wanted them to call him again. In that moment all I thought was, *I really hope this conversation ends soon. I want to go home and watch* Game of Thrones. How awful is that? These people were in deep pain and had come to me for consolation, but all I wanted was for them to leave.

I should have cared. Heck, it was my job to care. I should have provided pastoral counsel and prayer, at the least. But I didn't do any of that. I didn't care or help because I had done such a bad job of tending to my own mental health needs that I'd finally arrived at a place where it was nearly impossible for me to genuinely care much about anyone who wasn't my wife, my children, or myself. Doing work for the kingdom of Jesus at that point was all but out of the question. All I wanted was for my own pain to go away. And maybe to find out if the Mother of Dragons would sit on the Iron Throne. But that was about it.

How did I get so burned out?

I was coming off a period in life where I thought I could not only do everything but also needed to be everything to everyone all of the time. A friend said to me, "Ryan, I'm worried if you keep at the pace you're keeping, you're gonna crash, man. It's not sustainable." I thanked him politely for his concern. But do you know what I was thinking in my head? *Burnout is for losers. Guys like me don't burn out. Guys like me can't burn out.*

Oh, brother. There's a reason they say pride goes before the fall.

Instead of caring for myself I chose to charge ahead and remain focused on accomplishing my goals, in order to hopefully someday arrive at the good life. But I was in way over my head, overcommitted and undernourished. I could barely pray, hardly ever read my Bible except to prepare for sermons, and had begun—as you already know—to self-medicate my pain with alcohol and sleeping pills.

That's the thing about mental health. We can either tend to it, or we can ignore it and deal with the fallout, which is never good. The choice is ours. Because this choice is so incredibly important, I want to explore the concept of self-care from a Christian perspective. In the church, self-care is often seen as a hedonistic pursuit, but I would argue that taking care of our mental health is vital to our spiritual health.

I am aware that at first blush it might appear that sincere and intentional self-care is antithetical to Christianity. After all, our faith implores us to follow a self-sacrificing Christ, a man who told his followers that those who want to emulate his life must be willing to forfeit their own (Matt. 16:25). But what I'm advocating for here is something akin to the way the flight attendant instructs passengers to put their own masks on first if the airplane's cabin loses pressure. Our instinct is to reach out to help those in our care. But our instinct is wrong. For survival we must put our masks on first. Then (and only then) are we in a position to assist those with whom we're traveling. Putting your mask on first is not a selfish action. It is deeply Christian.

THE CALL TO LOVE

A teacher of the law tried to trip Jesus up. "Which is the greatest commandment?"

Jesus replied, as he often did, by quoting Scripture. On this occasion he drew from his memory of the book of Deuteronomy. Jesus said: "'Love the Lord your God with all your heart and with all your soul and with all your mind.' This is the first and greatest commandment. And the second is like it: 'Love your neighbor as yourself.' All the Law and the Prophets hang on these two commandments" (Matt. 22:36–40).

All of Christian teaching can be pared down to this: love God and love your neighbor. I think even the most casual observer of Christianity knows this about the religion. What is often missed, however, by both Christians and non-Christians alike, is the complexity of loving another as one loves oneself. On one level it's simple in that we inherently understand the challenge of extending strangers the kind of love we extend ourselves. Many of us spend inordinate amounts of time loving and providing for ourselves. Turning that level of devotion away from ourselves and out toward the person on the street is problematic but not conceptually impossible. But what if our love for self is twisted, highly compromised by trauma, or even nonexistent? What if, in fact, we hate ourselves? How then are we to understand the command to love others as ourselves?

It's been widely noted that we cannot give away what we don't already possess. Nowhere is this maxim truer than in the concept of love. Self-love is critical for love of others. People who cannot see and respect what is good and lovely in their own selves will have trouble seeing and loving what is loveable in others. This is also why knowing God is so difficult if we don't know ourselves. Scripture may tell us we are divinely made, but if we've never experienced the beauty of this divine design within us, it will be difficult, if not impossible, to love others as Jesus commands.

So much of Christian faith calls for our lives to be guided by the love Jesus exemplified on the cross, a self-sacrificial love. "Greater love has no one than this: to lay down one's life for one's friends" (John 15:13). In many respects this is what makes Christianity so uniquely powerful. It is a religion firmly rooted in its insistence that giving away oneself for the sake of others is the best way to live, the way that will bring everlasting peace and satisfaction in life. I believe this is true. I also believe this can't be done unless a self-love is first firmly established, one committed to taking care of our own mental health as part of our pursuit to love others well.

Notice something else often overlooked in the command of Jesus. We are not called to love our neighbors more than ourselves but to love our neighbors *as* ourselves. Hardly a good commandment for those who happen to hate themselves or are indifferent to self. The command, at that point, sort of loses its teeth, doesn't it? It follows then that we must first love and care for ourselves well if we are to offer our love in a helpful manner to others.

At the core of this is having a solid understanding of identity. That's where we must start on the road to Christian self-care. If we're going to be healthy then we have to know who we are.

IDENTITY IS A CHOICE

Shortly after I returned from in-patient rehab, my bishop hauled me into his office and abruptly asked, "Who do you understand yourself to be?"

I took a moment to consider the question before saying, "Well, I'm first and foremost a human being. I'm also a husband and a father—"

"No," he said, cutting me off. "You have a problem with chemicals. So, let's try this again. Who are you?"

I understood what he was getting at. He wanted me to say I was an alcoholic. He wanted me to see myself first and foremost as a problem drinker. The trouble was, his question hit at the very core of the primary issue I had been working on in therapy, but it ran in the wrong direction. In treatment I finally learned to stop couching my identity in anything other than my relationship to God. I finally came to terms with the fact that I suffer tremendously from the sin of pride, meaning I don't really believe I am enough as I am but rather that I need to earn my value by making myself worthy of admiration and love through achievement. Instead of accepting what God had already offered for free, I was bound and determined to make it costly and ultimately unattainable.

There is a reason the psalmist implored us to be still and know that God is God. The instruction is meant to guide us into a place of peace where we can trust in the Prince of Peace to provide all the identity we could ever need. But so long as we remain obsessed with "earning" our place in this life, we'll never truly be able to trust that we are God's beloved children—a status we did not earn and one we can never lose.

By the time I made it to the bishop's office that day I was finished measuring myself by what I did or did not do. In rehab I'd decided to no longer think of myself as a pastor or lawyer or therapist or writer. Likewise, I was not a problem drinker—not at my core. All of these words were simply descriptors of things I sometimes did and sometimes didn't do—not who I was.

Instead of continuing the endless chase for an identity of my own creation, I chose to model my life after Jesus, who was perfectly content to describe his identity solely in terms of his relationship to his heavenly Father: "The works that the Father has given me to finish—the very works that I am doing—testify that the Father has sent me" (John 5:36). That's who he was, and that's what his life was all about. The most important lesson I took away from rehab was that I was finished thinking of myself as anything but a beloved child of God. For it was only in that place—a place of total and radical acceptance—that I was able to find the strength I needed for the journey back toward health.

But this mentality didn't sit well with my bishop, nor did it with many of the people I encountered in Alcoholics Anonymous, for grace is hard to accept. I'll never forget the first AA meeting I attended. It was a large men's group that had been meeting in the same church for years. The camaraderie in the room was palpable, as loud laughter and bear hugs erupted each time another man walked through the door. I was awestruck by how genuinely happy these men were, and I couldn't help but wonder if the Christians who attended this church on Sunday entered with the same level of enthusiasm.

If you've never been to an AA meeting, you've most likely seen one portrayed in the movies and you know that when people introduce themselves, they do so in a very particular manner, saying, "Hi, I'm so-and-so, and I'm an alcoholic." In some meetings they'll also add the date of their sobriety or acknowledge they're returning to the group after a "slipup." Even though I had never attended an AA meeting, I had studied its philosophy and knew the only real requirement for attending a closed meeting was to have a desire not to drink. When I went to this meeting, I was incredibly worried about my drinking, was abstaining from alcohol, and was committed to doing so for the foreseeable future. But was I an alcoholic? I honestly didn't know. What I did know was that I wasn't ready to call myself one.

When it came time for me to introduce myself to the hundred or so men gathered in the large circle, I said, with a tremble in my voice, "Hi, I'm Ryan, and I'm trying to figure out whether I'm an alcoholic."

For a moment it felt as though the air had been sucked out of the room. I mostly looked at the floor, but I felt as though I had somehow stained the brotherhood by not fully embracing the identity of the group. I wasn't certain I belonged, and I wanted to be honest about this fact. When the meeting ended, several men gave me their business cards and encouraged me to call them for a cup of coffee. I know their efforts were nothing but sincere, but I couldn't help but feel as though I was being pressured to adopt an identity they were certain would be good for me. The subtext to these conversations implied it would only be a matter of time until I realized this truth about myself. The longer I denied my identity as an alcoholic, the greater danger I placed myself in. I think this is what my bishop also believed.

I continued attending these sorts of meetings for a long time, eventually adopting the standard protocol for introducing myself. "Hi," I would say, "I'm Ryan, and I'm an alcoholic." But it never felt true to me—not in my bones. Did I have a problem with drinking? Absolutely. Do I still have a complicated relationship with drinking? Yes, I do. Have I gone for long periods of time without consuming any alcohol? Yes, I have done that. Have I also consumed alcohol responsibly for long stretches of time? Yup. But have I also had instances where I have once again abused alcohol while trying to consume responsibly? Yeah, I've unfortunately done that too.

Nevertheless, asking me to understand myself as an alcoholic as the basis of my identity is just not helpful to me because it confuses my fundamental grounding in God as the source of my identity. A word of clarification: for millions of people, identifying as an alcoholic or an addict is a lifesaving act. Acknowledging this aspect of their identity really does keep them out of harm's way. I once read that legendary screenwriter Aaron Sorkin said the hardest thing he does every day is stay sober. I know a lot of people like that. If they place anything before their sobriety, everything else falls apart. Consequently, marking themselves with an identity associated to drinking or drug use is an absolute must. To that person, I say, more power to you. I am in no way advocating that anyone who finds healing by identifying with an addiction stop doing so.

What I am saying is that, for me, I am not a depressive *first*. Nor am I a problem drinker *first*. Before I am anything, I am a beloved child of God. If I try and understand myself in any other way, things go sideways on me. I choose to root my identity in the one described in Scripture, where we're told that all humans were created first and foremost in the image of God (Gen. 1:27). Taken seriously, this means that every other identity we attach to ourselves—husband,

wife, CEO, athlete, artist, even Christian—must come after our iden-
tification as a human being God willingly chose to create and love.

Any person in any kind of sustained recovery understands how
important it is to own your truth. My truth is that I cannot identify
as anything or anyone beyond who God created me to be: his child. I
must have this identity buried in my bones because I will inevitably
fail to live into and up to my other self-constructed or societally
imposed identities. I will rebel from the teachings of Jesus. I will
be unfaithful, either in heart or action, to my wife. I will lose a job.
I *have* lost a job. I will let my physical health fall by the wayside. I
will disappoint a friend or one of my children. When these things
occur, I will be in danger of an identity crisis if I have made any one
of these secondary identities my primary identity.

But if I know that I am a child who has a Father in heaven who
has promised me that nothing I can do will ever separate me from
his love, then I'm positioned to not only take care of myself well
but to also bounce back from any kind of devastating experience. I
can trust my fate does not rest in my ability but in the promise of a
Father who never fails to provide his children with what they need.

HOW QUICKLY WE FORGET

I believe, deep down, we know the truth about where we come from
and whose we are, but over time we forget. Have you ever watched
a child's reaction when you promise to tell them about the day they
were born? They suddenly get very still and quiet. *You know about
my past?* their eyes seem to ask. *You know things I can't remember?*

They'll hang on every word you say.

In his book, *Immortal Diamond*, Richard Rohr shared a story

I have never been able to forget. I have no idea if the story actually happened. Neither does Rohr. All I know is that it is true in the greatest sense of the word. The story goes something like this.

A young couple has two children, a four-year-old and a new-born. One evening they're putting the newborn to bed when the four-year-old says, "I want to talk to the baby!"

"Go ahead," the parents say. "He's right here. Say whatever you like."

"No," the boy says. "I want to talk to the baby by myself."

Curious about the request for secrecy, the parents agree. They invite the four-year-old into the nursery, place the baby in his crib, and leave the room. Spying at the door, this is what they see and hear:

The boy creeps up to the crib and whispers, "Quick, tell me where you came from. Quick, tell me who made you. I'm beginning to forget."[1]

I'm beginning to forget. Don't you love that?

I think infants are born with knowledge of God. I think that's the special spark we see in their eyes. Some people say it's innocence, but I think it's something even better than that. I think it's knowl-edge. Children know that what matters most is not what they do in life but who they are in God.

The question is, do we?

TRUE IDENTITY LEADS TO OUR TRUE DESTINY

In an ideal setting a Christian community acts as a holy place of refuge. As such it attracts troubled people, folks experiencing pain, financial crisis, illness, domestic violence, addiction. Name one of the gnarlier life waves we humans ride, and you'll find someone in the pews wiping out on it. Or rather, you *should* find that. After all, Jesus was more than a bit concerned with those on the margins of society—those with struggles, those the establishment would rather ignore or treat as less than. The ceremoniously unclean (nonreligious), women (property), children (worthless until proven worthy), and traitorous men (tax collectors). The people our society calls addict, poor, bigot, greedy, lazy, stupid, sinner, and selfish were Jesus' people. Consequently, as Christians, they must be our people, especially if we're conceiving of our entire lives as one great journey back to God.

Here's the rub. These margin folks, the ones for whom extra grace might be required, are our brothers and sisters in Christ. But they're also the people who might cause us to say, *Jesus Christ!* And not in the nice way. And look, I say this as one who not only ministers to this crew but also belongs to this crew. I thank God for the folks who are willing to show me grace.

When I was first discerning a call to ordained ministry, I sought out the counsel of a friend's father who'd been a Lutheran minister for more than twenty years. I wanted to know about his career, whether he was fulfilled, and what I might expect should I choose a similar path. He was helpful on several levels, but it was this question that got burned into my brain: "Ryan," he said, "how do you do spending time with people you'd rather not?"

His question stuck because the longer I worked in ministry, the more I understood how much ministry involves making ourselves available for people we'd rather not spend time with. Yes, we preach sermons, fundraise, plan Vacation Bible Schools, and fling missionaries off to the far corners of the world to proclaim the gospel, which is all fine and good and valuable. But the heart of what the church does, or should be doing, is making space for folks who haven't found space anywhere else. I believe this is the holiest call of the church because it most closely mirrors the life of Christ, a dude who just couldn't leave people behind, not even the thieves and onlookers who mocked him while dying on a Roman cross. Jesus *always* made room for another person to join his tribe and then told us to go and do the same.

This call is not only for those in "official" ministry positions. It is a principle all Christians ought to adopt. I grew up in the Baptist tradition where the priesthood of all believers was a doctrine we took very seriously. This doctrine says that it doesn't matter if someone is a plumber or the pastor of a megachurch. Everyone who chooses to follow Jesus carries the same burden and mission to proclaim the gospel with the entirety of their lives. All of us are called to lay down our lives, pick up our crosses, and follow after Jesus. But for that to happen in healthy ways, we must first learn how to take our own self-care seriously.

As mentioned before, it is no small matter to adopt an outlook on life that calls you to love your neighbor as yourself and pray for your enemy. If we want to have any hope of living into these imperatives, we first must take care of and love ourselves. And there is no way, I believe, we'll be able to do this unless we find our identity in knowing we are God's forever beloved children. Otherwise, we're toast.

Loving and partnering with people we dislike (and might even fear) isn't always easy. It really should come as no surprise that our holiest calling is also our most difficult one. Caring for the wounded takes a toll on our minds, bodies, and spirits. Ask caregivers how they stay healthy, and they'll most likely talk about caring for themselves *first*.

Loving yourself comes naturally when the brain and soul are

working in harmony. The image of God planted within us, combined with our evolutionarily developed instinct for survival, serves our desire for self-preservation and joy. Inherently, we take care of ourselves and treat ourselves to the wonders of life. But mental illness complicates all of this. And not just mental illnesses—a more mundane mental health struggle, like loneliness or the challenge of a job transition, can also bring about the conditions that make self-love more difficult. Prioritizing mental health is one of the best ways to protect the psyche from the pitfalls of any one of these situations.

For too long we have asked Christians to soldier on displaying the love of Christ without making sure they first understand how to love themselves. We need to encourage individuals to explore the various needs and desires they have in their hearts in order for them to be well positioned to become the most alive versions of themselves. This is what Saint Irenaeus, the second-century bishop of Lyons, meant when he said that the glory of God is men and women who are fully alive, fully human. So much of contemporary Christianity emphasizes following rules and conforming our beliefs around correct doctrine that we neglect the uniqueness of each individual and the fact that God has placed diverse longings in each and every one of our hearts.

In his book, *Soulful Spirituality: Becoming Fully Alive and Deeply Human*, David Benner recounted the following tale I find illustrative for our need to become ourselves:

One day a spiritual teacher asked his disciples why God made humans. One of them—an eager man—answered almost immediately, "That, teacher, is easy. So we can pray." After a brief silence, the teacher asked another question: "Why, then, did God make angels?" The same young man tried again, "Perhaps so that they also could pray." The teacher looked at him and smiled. "The angels," he said, "are perfectly capable of offering prayer to God, but only humans can do what they are uniquely created to do." "What is that?" the eager disciple asked. "What God wants from humans and what only humans can do is become fully human."[2]

Allowing yourself the freedom to pursue desire is a fantastic way to ward off self-loathing and develop self-love. Engaging in activities you find enjoyable is one way of showing yourself that you matter and are loved. For whatever reason, it's easy to conceive of this notion when providing it for other people but more difficult when doing it for ourselves. But doing it for ourselves is precisely what needs to be done. Think of it this way: if you say you love someone but never show your love in action, that person is likely to become suspicious of your protestations of love. It's like the husband who professes he'd take a bullet for his wife but can't be bothered to open her car door. His words ring hollow. The same goes for you. It's not enough to tell yourself that you are loved. You must show yourself this love in action. Otherwise, you won't really believe it because even though your mind has thought it, your body will not have felt it.

I recently went through another two-week depressive period that was particularly severe. For whatever reason, my thought pattern turned toxic, and my brain once again became my worst enemy. No matter what I did or said, my inner critic told me I was dumb and worthless. It was bad; I was stuck in a downward spiral I simply could not get out of. My self-love tank was on empty. Finally, I decided I'd had enough, so I tried an experiment.

One morning I simply made the decision that I was going to be nice to myself. So whenever I had a thought that wasn't nice, I called it out for what it was—unkind—and then I dismissed it. I did this all day and it was a ton of work because my thoughts were in full onslaught mode. But here's the thing. By the time I went to bed that evening, I felt more at peace than I had in weeks. Had my depression totally lifted? No. But I felt much, much better because I'd actually done something to remind my body that I was loved. I protected myself from myself, which sometimes is the most powerful kind of self-love that exists.

In her wonderful book *The Gifts of Imperfection*, Brené Brown wrote about how she once asked her blog readers what they thought about the importance of loving themselves and the idea that we can't love other people more than we love ourselves. A heated debate broke out in the comments section. Some commentators did not believe people need to love themselves in order to love others. Others, however, pointed out that by loving ourselves we can learn how to love others. Brown shared in her book two comments that "addressed the complexity of these ideas in straightforward terms." I have reprinted one of them for you below. It comes from a mental health professional named Justin Valentin, who wrote:

> Through my children I have learned to really love unconditionally, to be compassionate at times when I am feeling horrible, and to be so much more giving. When I look at my one daughter who looks so much like me, I can see myself in that little girl. This reminds me to be kinder to the little girl that lives inside me and to love and accept her as my own. It is the love for my girls that makes me want to be a better person and to work on loving and accepting myself. However, with that being said, it is still so much easier to love my daughters. . . .
>
> Perhaps thinking about it this way makes more sense: Many

of my patients are mothers who struggle with drug addiction.... They destroy their lives, hate themselves, and often damage their bodies beyond repair ... but they love their children. They believe their children are lovable, but they believe they are unlovable. On the surface, one might say [that] some of them love their children more than themselves. However, does loving your children mean that you are not intentionally poisoning them the way you poison yourself? Perhaps our issues are like secondhand smoke ... [which] can be very deadly.[3]

What this comment illustrates for me is that true love will only spring forth in lasting ways from people who are intent on caring for themselves. The secondhand smoke image is brilliant. It is a mistake to believe that what I do or do not do to me only affects me. If I do not love myself, this lack of love will eventually affect my ability to love others. The love I set out to give will not be given because there will be nothing within me to give. God has graciously given us life. We must love this life we have been offered freely before we can freely offer love to anyone else, otherwise we will have cheapened the gift.

Again, the best model for this kind of self-love is Jesus himself. Over and again in the gospels we find Jesus retreating from the large crowds following him to be alone and pray. Jesus wasn't doing this just to be pious and set a good example for the disciples. He was engaging in self-love by doing the thing he most wanted to do in life: talking with his father. Can we do any less as we seek to follow our own divine calling?

*T*he plan is for you to go away for a time, find healing, and then hopefully return to your duties at the church in four months where your job will be waiting for you. Not only that, you will continue to receive your full salary and medical benefits while you are away. Your family is secure. You breathe a sigh of relief. The church could have fired you on the spot. You are grateful for their generosity. You are also horribly worried about your wife and the two young children you are leaving her to care for on her own. It's not that you don't think she can do it. She can. She is the strongest, most capable woman you have ever known. Still, the guilt is enormous. She shouldn't have to be doing this.

One week passes, then it is time to go. Your wife shows unimaginable strength and optimism in the face of what's coming, and you have never been more grateful for her love and indefatigable character. You can do this, she tells you. Go and fight for yourself so you can come back and fight for us like you always have. She doesn't want you to worry about her or the children. She will make it. She can do this. She reminds you that a lot of her friends' husbands travel constantly for work. She paints this as an extended work trip. That is all.

You want to believe her. You try to believe her. You know that she will make it—and not just make it but make it well. She's that kind of woman. Her loyalty to you and the *children is unmatched, and she'll do whatever it takes to make sure everyone feels loved and provided for in your absence. She is better than you. She is the best person you have ever known. But this will be a long stretch. Everyone is scared.*

The morning comes, and you weep uncontrollably in one another's arms, trying hard not to wake the children. Then you go and kiss them goodbye in their beds. The oldest wakes up. The two of you share some private and sacred words. And you leave determined to do whatever you need to do in order to never find yourself back in this situation again.

TEN

TALK THERAPY

Most people don't have a good map for navigating the winding roads of mental illness. Unless you've witnessed a family member or close friend deal with these issues up close, they can feel as foreign and disorienting as any experience imaginable. From our earliest days, we have been told what to do if we catch the common cold: rest and drink plenty of fluids. The same goes for a sprained ankle: head to the doctor for an X-ray. But when depression or anxiety strikes, the avenues toward healing are far less obvious.

I saw this firsthand when I was working as a pastor. Time and again, members of the congregation would come to my office seeking prayer for issues that were spiritual (what isn't?) but also sounded like they warranted professional attention. I heard stories about difficulty getting out of bed in the morning. Others described an inability to fall asleep at night. Some couldn't control their drinking. Some were engaging in destructive and illegal behavior like visiting sex workers or using illegal drugs. Some no longer wanted to live.

I would always pray with them and offer whatever wisdom I

could glean from the Bible and the Christian tradition, but my suggestion that they also seek counseling was most often met with a tepid response that they would "look into it." When I'd circle back with these folks to see if they'd taken me up on seeing a therapist, the answer was almost always a sheepish no. When I inquired further as to why they hadn't sought help, I discovered they found the task of seeking professional help to be overwhelming. Most just didn't know where to start. They didn't know what kind of therapist to call. They didn't know which sorts of therapists specialized in which kinds of problems. They didn't know if their insurance would cover the cost. Perhaps most importantly, many worried God would judge them for needing this kind of help.

In these instances, I would do my best to explain that seeking help for mental health is no different from seeking help for physical health, but rarely was I successful in changing anyone's mind. My failure to convince many Christians of the merit of psychological aid was one of the primary reasons I decided to go back to school and become a mental health professional. I desperately wanted other Christians to discover the help I had found on the couch of a therapist, and I thought that if I gained an understanding of not just what it meant to be a patient but also a provider, I might be a more effective evangelist for the mental health-care field.

If you've ever found yourself generally confused about which path to take to address your mental health, I hope to provide some answers in the following chapters about the practical steps you can take to find the healing you need. Because no two mental illnesses present in the exact same way, it's also true that no two people find healing in exactly the same way. The paths toward healing are as diverse as the diverse brains, souls, and bodies these maladies invade. Given this reality, I would like to offer up a three-legged stool approach that I have found helpful in not only my own life but also in the lives of many others.

The three legs to my stool for treating mental illness are *talk therapy*, *medication*, and *people*. Let's start by discussing talk therapy, which was usually my first recommendation for the folks who came to my office. Then we'll move on to the wonders of modern medicine and the unrivaled support we can find in a strong network of people who love and care for us.

LET'S TALK THERAPY

When I first went and got help years ago, it felt all kinds of awkward. I'm not going to lie to you: if you've never seen a therapist before, sitting down on a couch when you feel like the absolute worst version of yourself and then having someone ask you to talk about *why* you feel this way can feel far more akin to torture than treatment. All I really wanted to do at that point was roll up into the fetal position and hide out in my bedroom. But this guy, this doctor, wanted me to talk about my relationship with my mother and how much alcohol I drank and whether I really enjoyed my job and found my marriage fulfilling. No big deal, right?

It felt difficult and scary and nutty all at the same time. And it was expensive. I can't tell you how many times I left his office in those early days thinking, *I can't believe I'm paying for this. I really must be crazy.*

But guess what? With time, I discovered that talking about what was going on inside me was exactly what I needed. Processing my life—past, current, and the hopeful future—somehow started to make me feel better. It's difficult to pinpoint where the magic lies in therapy, but for me I think it was having the space to truly be vulnerable about all that I was thinking and feeling without judgment. Having a trained professional give you undivided attention is an enormously powerful thing. Having the guarantee that the person will not judge you is even better.

I felt safe with my therapist, so we got to work. And it changed my life. Over time, what had felt like insurmountable problems began to feel more manageable. Was my life suddenly perfect? No, of course not. I mean, you already know I ran into more trouble later on. But when I started therapy I began healing in ways I previously never had. It felt miraculous.

So when I say that I highly recommend therapy as a tool if you're struggling with mental health, I say it from personal experience. I know how awkward and confusing and scary it can be both to acknowledge you need help and to start the healing journey, much less to wade into the unknown waters of therapy. But I can tell you it's worth it in more ways than I can count. So why don't we wade in together? Let's talk about the questions you might have and get you on your way.

WHAT ARE SOME OF THE BENEFITS OF TALK THERAPY?

It would be impossible to list every benefit a person might receive from therapy, but the list below represents a few of the most commonly cited.

Access to a safe space and safe person.

It's difficult to overemphasize the value of knowing you can go to the same office at the same time to speak with the same person about anything and everything in your heart and mind. Introducing this kind of consistency into a person's life through talk therapy, in and of itself, can be life-changing. When else do you have the opportunity to receive a person's undivided attention for a full fifty minutes or longer? And not just any person, but one who has spent years learning how to listen and reflect and guide in ways that are in your best interest with no other motive than to see you become the healthiest version of yourself?

Improved psychology.

Healthy thinking leads to healthy living. The more time we spend understanding how we interpret the events of our lives, the more able we will be to make whatever adjustments are needed to correct faulty thinking and feel better about ourselves. We are not a product of our feelings. We always have a choice.

Improved brain functioning.

Parts of our brains are highly elastic, meaning they are open to changing patterns and making new connections. One of the best parts about talk therapy is that it can help the brain do this, with or without the help of medication. Using brain-imaging methods, psychotherapy has been shown to alter activity in the medial prefrontal cortex, the anterior cingulate cortex, the hippocampus, and the amygdala. These areas are involved in self-referential thoughts, executive control, emotion, and fear. Who doesn't need help with those things?

Improved coping skills.

Learning to manage stress and anxiety in healthy manners should be just as important in school as learning to read and write. Unfortunately, most people were never explicitly taught how to manage stress and other negative feelings. In therapy, we can learn to identify what coping mechanisms we're already using and examine whether healthier mechanisms should be learned and implemented.

Improved ability to recognize triggers.

Sometimes we don't know exactly what is causing unwanted feelings or behaviors in our lives. We know there must be something, but we can't quite put our finger on it. Allowing a therapist to listen to the patterns of your life can be one of the most valuable aspects of therapy because they're trained to recognize triggers and help you identify how to better handle or avoid them.

Improved physical health.

Psychological trauma often triggers physical pain when left unprocessed. Processing this trauma in therapy often ameliorates physical symptoms like stomachaches, headaches, ulcers, and insomnia.

HOW DO I GO ABOUT FINDING A THERAPIST?

While Google can be your best friend for reading breaking news or instantly settling an argument about who was the twenty-third president of the United States, it can feel overwhelming to rely on the famed search engine when looking for a therapist. Fortunately, there are better ways. Here are six of them:

1. Ask family and friends.

People are often surprised to learn their friends and family not only know of reputable therapists in their area but have been in therapy themselves for years. One of the ways to discover a good therapist is to simply ask the people you trust most in life. Asking about a therapist is also a good way to strengthen your support network, as it lets people know you might be going through a difficult season of life.

2. Ask your primary care physician.

Your doctor is one of the best resources you have when it comes to finding a good therapist. Local therapists market themselves to primary care physicians for this very purpose, knowing full well that doctors get asked for therapist recommendations frequently. More importantly, a primary care physician typically sees a high volume of patients, meaning he or she not only has made lots of referrals but also has worked with patients long enough to receive feedback as to which therapists have proven helpful and which ones have not.

3. Contact your local university's psychiatry or psychology department.

Many of these programs will have clinics on campus where student therapists provide services at low to no cost. Reputable programs will have fully licensed clinicians monitoring the student therapists closely to ensure they're providing proper care.

4. Ask your clergy.

Reams of research suggest this is what most people do when faced with a mental health crisis. This can be helpful if you're hoping to find a therapist who aligns with your particular denomination or faith tradition. Ideally, your church will keep an updated list of trusted referrals in the area. Call the church and ask. A word of warning: If you suspect your church's theology to be hostile to therapy, tread lightly. I have seen a lot of damage done by well-meaning but misinformed pastors when it comes to discussing the merits of psychotherapy.

5. Call your insurance provider.

This is the fastest way to find out which therapists in your area are in-network for you, which means they'll accept your insurance.

6. Search the *Psychology Today* website.

Psychology Today's website is great because of its widespread use by therapists across the country and because it allows therapists to express themselves with bios and photos to give potential clients a sense of their personality, theoretical orientation, and years of experience. Therapists also display their credentials, license numbers, and links to their personal or business websites. Many also indicate their fee or fee range to provide a sense of affordability.

WHAT IS THE DIFFERENCE BETWEEN THE VARIOUS TYPES OF THERAPISTS?

No matter where I go to speak about mental health, I always get asked this question: Can you briefly explain the differences between the types of therapists out there? In answer, I've compiled the short list below. While not totally comprehensive, it does cover the bulk of mental health professionals in the United States.

Psychiatrists

Psychiatrists are medical doctors (MDs or DOs) who specialize in the diagnosis, treatment, and prevention of mental illnesses, with some specializing in addiction. Among the many treatments they employ are medication, talk therapy, and brain stimulation. As medical doctors, they can also quickly identify when a patient might be experiencing a mental health episode as a result of a physical symptom that should immediately be explored by another medical doctor with expertise in that field. Given the rigorous training doctors go through in medical school, residency, and other fellowships and opportunities to specialize their practices, psychiatrists often make fantastic mental health professionals, especially for patients suffering from some of the more serious illnesses like schizophrenia, bipolar disorder, or anorexia nervosa.

Most who practice psychiatry minimize the role of the soul (if not discount it entirely) to focus on matters of the body. Consequently, their practices tend to revolve around treating mental illness by way of medication and other medical procedures. Some psychiatrists continue to practice talk therapy, but they are becoming few and far between.

Psychiatric Mental Health Nurses

Psychiatric mental health nurses work with individuals, families, groups, and communities, assessing and helping to treat their mental health needs by offering direct care. These nurses have masters' degrees and in some cases doctoral degrees. Given the current shortage of psychiatrists in the United States, these PMHNs fill a unique gap in that they have a wide range of tools in their toolbox with which to work. They can provide education; conduct psychotherapy; prescribe medication; diagnose, treat, and manage chronic mental illnesses; order, perform, and interpret medical lab tests; conduct physical examinations; and perform certain medical procedures.

Psychologists

Psychologists are doctorate-level (PhD or PsyD) mental health professionals with varying degrees of training and expertise. Most psychologists have attended a four- or five-year program after earning their masters' degrees, which includes a one-year post-doc assignment, much like a physician's residency. Psychologists do a lot of talk therapy but are also proficient in providing testing for learning differences, such as ADHD, or administering IQ tests. Currently, only psychologists in the military, Iowa, Idaho, Louisiana, New Mexico, Illinois, and the Indian Health Service have the power to write prescriptions for mental health medications. It should also be noted that there are different kinds of psychologists: clinical psychologists, counseling psychologists, organizational psychologists, and school psychologists.

Clinical Social Workers, Licensed Professional Counselors, and Marriage and Family Therapists

Clinical social workers, licensed professional counselors, and marriage and family therapists are typically master's-level clinicians (although some have doctorates) who provide counseling to both individuals and families. They are trained to treat serious mental illnesses, substance use disorders, family conflict, eating disorders, sexual disorders, and more through therapy and advocacy. In most states, LPCs and LMFTs must perform three thousand hours of supervised training post conferral of their master's degree to become independently licensed.

HOW DO I CHOOSE THE RIGHT THERAPIST FOR ME?

Besides finding a therapist who speaks your language and has offices in a location you can reasonably travel to, the following three factors can be used as a guide for making an informed decision once you've narrowed down the type of mental health professional you need to see.

Credentials

Not every helping professional is licensed by a governing board. Ideally, they would be. That's not to say an unlicensed life coach can't be helpful—many are—it's only to say you run a greater risk by submitting to treatment from an individual who is not held accountable to some form of peer-reviewed group. The real danger is when a mental health professional falsely claims to have a license. Fortunately, these situations can be quickly remedied by Google searches.

Each state carries the burden for licensing mental health professionals, and they all do it a little differently. But what they all have are up-to-date websites that list who's who and whether a person's license is active or if anyone has filed grievances against that person. This is another point in the column for using a licensed professional because the system for discipline is transparent and the public can easily be made aware of any issues the therapist has had in the past. It's never a bad idea to verify a credential. Most mental health professionals list their numbers on their websites, business cards, and even social media accounts.

Expertise

Not all therapists are created equal. While not always a hard and fast rule, there is usually a direct correlation between a therapist's experience and effectiveness. In other words, if you get to choose, go with the therapist who has worked for a few years as opposed to the kid who's still a little too proud of earning the degree. Beyond years in the field, it's helpful to inquire about a particular therapist's interest and specialty training. Some therapists operate as general practitioners, but many specialize their practice over the years and stay more up to date on certain issues or modalities.

For instance, if you want to explore your fear of riding elevators, then you most likely want a therapist who is trained in cognitive behavioral therapy and knows a thing or two about exposure therapy. Moreover, if your issue has to do with understanding your sexual orientation within a Christian worldview, it won't do you much good to find a therapist who isn't comfortable with either sex or religion. Most therapists these days build out their websites in an effort to distinguish themselves from others by describing their philosophy and interests. Doing a little research can get you a lot.

Connection

What actually matters most as you're choosing the right therapist is the relational connection you feel with that person. That is to say, the one factor that is most determinative for whether therapy will be helpful is the level of comfort and trust formed between you and your therapist. Beyond theoretical approach or technique, there is nothing more important for healing than the therapeutic relationship itself. For a client to show up fully in the presence of a therapist who is able to accept the client—so-called warts and all—will be the single most significant vehicle for change.

The curative nature of the therapist-client relationship is so important that tending to it is usually just as important as the content processed during sessions. The reason for this is that the therapist-client relationship, when functioning well, acts as a microcosm for what the client's other relationships look like. This means the client begins to interact with the therapist in ways that are similar to how the client interacts with everyone else. This displacement of feelings onto the therapist is called *transference* and is one of the most important concepts in understanding why psychotherapy is so effective.

For example, as the client works with the therapist and experiences feelings of anger or sadness or love for the therapist, the client can also, with time, begin to recognize that these feelings can't actually be directed toward the therapist, who has done nothing to provoke them. Rather, the feelings and emotions were already present and being brought into all other relationships. Raising these feelings and emotions to the client's level of awareness is helpful in understanding how and why they operate in the client's life.

The relationship between therapist and client is also crucial because talk therapy requires vulnerability on the part of the client. A client who does not feel safe with a therapist is unlikely to get much out of the sessions. Most people greatly fear being judged by their therapist, but once they realize the therapist's only desire is to create a space where anything can be said in hopes of having a space where anything can be healed, this fear of judgment melts away quickly.

How do you make sure you're not months into therapy before you realize the connection with your therapist isn't right? Many mental health professionals will allow for a no-cost consultation phone call. I suggest you do this if it's an option. While not always accurate, human beings have an innate sense for knowing whether we'll get along with another person very quickly. Warmth, tone, interest, skill level, and curiosity are all qualities that can often be discerned on a phone call.

Beyond the initial call, try and view the first session as an interview where you are not simply coming to the expert for help but also assessing whether you believe the therapist can help you. For any number of reasons, you and the therapist may not work together.

Do your best to not feel obligated to continue the treatment if you don't believe it's in your best interest. Ideally, with some legwork, you will find a therapist you can trust and feel fully accepted by, thereby making the work of unveiling yourself that much easier and more productive.

To get you started down this road, here are some potential questions to ask during a consultation phone call or email thread:

1. Do you have a particular orientation to therapy?
2. Do you primarily see adults, adolescents, or children?
3. Do you take insurance?
4. What is your fee? Do you accept a sliding scale?
5. How long have you been in practice?
6. Are you faith based? If not, are you comfortable working with faith-based clients?
7. Are you comfortable working with someone in the LGBTQ community?

HOW DO I PAY FOR THERAPY?

Therapy can be an expensive endeavor. Therapists, like all professionals, must earn a living wage that both provides for their needs and accurately reflects the level of time and money invested into the development of their career. That said, there are many ways to find affordable treatment. Let's look at them.

Private Pay

In this scenario, the client agrees to pay a certain fee for each session, which is typically due at the time of service. Depending on the skill and reputation of the therapist, the fee may be set, or, to make room for clients with a lower income or for a client who might be experiencing temporary financial distress, the fee might be lowered.

A tip for potential clients: a fee can always be negotiated. Never let a high fee dissuade you from trying to work with a therapist if you think that therapist will be helpful to you. While I can't guarantee it will get you anywhere, it's always worth asking if your therapist of choice works on a sliding scale. Personally, I try my hardest to never let money keep me from working with a client who is a good fit. Most therapists I know are guided by a similar principle. After all, we didn't get into this business to get rich, but to help people.

Insurance

Using insurance to pay for counseling can be great. Instead of paying a clinician's full fee, you pay only the copay, just like you do when visiting your medical doctor, and your insurance company picks up the rest of the tab. The drawback here is the therapist will have to make a diagnosis in order for insurance to reimburse. So, if you want to keep a mental health diagnosis out of your medical record, don't use insurance to pay for therapy.

Subscription Service

Increasingly, people are engaging in therapy online. Most mental health professionals are now authorized by their respective boards to offer online services to clients who reside in their state. These sessions take place on the phone or via other HIPAA-approved platforms that operate similarly to a video call.

Capitalizing on this technological revolution are app-based companies like BetterHelp and Talkspace, which employ vast networks of therapists all across the country. Most of these apps operate on a subscription fee that is due monthly and can be cancelled at any time. These services can be great for people who are in rural areas, are homebound, or suffer from agoraphobia (fear of going outside).

Clinics, Colleges, and Hospitals

If you are uninsured and low on funds, look up local clinics, colleges, and hospitals. It is highly likely that these institutions will offer low- or no-cost therapy from therapists in training.

ONCE I'VE SETTLED ON A THERAPIST, WHAT CAN I EXPECT FROM THE FIRST SESSION AND BEYOND?

The way talk therapy usually works is a client comes in for an initial appointment and expresses the reason for seeking out therapy. A good therapist will listen carefully and make an initial assessment as to whether the client is in crisis. If the therapist determines the client needs an immediate intervention, be it hospitalization or in-patient treatment of some kind, this suggestion will be made immediately. Otherwise, the therapist will proceed with what is known as the intake interview.

This interview looks a lot like what you experience at the doctor's office when the nurse comes in and asks you a bunch of questions before the doctor sees you. The interview can feel invasive because, depending on the therapist, you may be asked questions about family history, drug use, alcohol consumption, sexual orientation, job history, and financial status. What's important to remember is that the intake interview is not a litmus test. The questions aren't asked so the therapist can make a judgment about the client but more so to determine how best to help.

Once the intake interview is complete, and if both client and therapist believe the relationship might be fruitful, they proceed with the sessions, typically meeting weekly or biweekly. The conversations that follow are not casual, rambling chats as often depicted on television but thoughtfully guided explorations into whatever the presenting issues are.

No two therapists do this in the exact same manner. Some ask direct questions to get the ball rolling while others choose to sit back and wait to see what the client chooses to bring up in the session. The therapy continues for as long as it is productive for the client. Depending on the circumstances, this could mean the relationship lasts only a few sessions while others remain in therapy with the same therapist for years.

Again, there is no one-size-fits-all approach. That said, it is incumbent on the therapist to not keep a client in therapy any longer than is beneficial for the client. Therapists have an ethical obligation to terminate therapy when goals have been reached, the client wishes to terminate, or the therapist is no longer in a position to be effective.

THERE IS HELP

One of the hardest aspects of mental illness is feeling like you are all alone and nobody understands what you are going through. But the reality is, there are millions who not only understand but are trained and ready to help you walk through it. I remember when I first enrolled in my counseling program and came home from class telling my wife that almost everyone I met who was already in the profession or training to join it had so much compassion. Never had I been around so many people who were passionately committed to devoting their lives to helping other people. It was inspiring.

One of the things that breaks my heart the most when people deny themselves therapy is that they are missing out on benefiting not only from evidence-based treatments but also from interacting with some of the most loving, open-minded, and selfless people in the world.

When I was going through an intensive out-patient treatment program after I returned from in-patient, I worked with a therapist who was about my age and was also a Christian. Together we spent a lot of our time talking about what it meant for me to be a pastor who had taken such a far fall from grace. In my mind what I had done disqualified me from ever taking any kind of leadership role again. In some ways, I wasn't sure I even deserved to call myself a Christian; that's how bad I felt about what I had done. This kind man sat and listened for hours and hours as I bemoaned my situation and lamented about the mistakes of my past. One morning we were sitting together, and he said, "Ryan, do you know that nothing you have done disqualifies you from serving Jesus?"

"Oh, yes, it does," I replied. "I have no business ever serving Christ in his church again. I blew that opportunity."

My therapist just sat with a warm look on his face and stared at me for a long time. Finally, he said, "I've never told you this, but a long time ago I was dismissed from a leadership position in the church." I was shocked. I hadn't even known he ever worked in a church. He continued, "It was the most devastating experience of my life. I felt like my entire identity had been robbed. I felt like I had let down God. I literally had no idea who I was anymore, and it took me a long, long time to heal from it."

"But you healed?" I asked. "I mean, were you able to get over it?"

He smiled softly. "In time, yeah, I was."

"How?"

"Because even though I was dismissed from the church, I was never dismissed from God. In my darkest moment, when I was cut off from the body of Christ, I discovered that Christ hadn't cut me off and that he never would. What was done was done. My own Good Friday had come, but Jesus hung in there next to me and promised Easter was on the way. And he was right."

My therapist didn't have to reveal himself in that way to me. He was under no obligation to share with me something very painful from his past, but he did it anyway because he knew it would be helpful to me. For that I will be forever grateful.

What is so beautiful about the men and women who commit themselves to doing this kind of work is that they show up each day not only prepared to share their expertise but also the innermost chambers of their hearts, all in an effort to do whatever it takes to help those of us who are sick become well once again.

You are not alone in these illnesses. There is help out there—really excellent help. Don't deprive yourself of its benefits without at least trying it out. Remember, mental illness does not discriminate, but therapy just might save your life.

It did for me.

It does for me still.

ELEVEN

MEDICATION

At first I refused the drugs. I was one of those Christians utterly convinced that taking a mental health medication amounted to a failing of faith. It's not like I thought Jesus would turn his back on me if I used an antidepressant, but there was something shameful about accepting the reality that I needed a pill to bring peace to my mind while also professing faith in the Prince of Peace. And so, even though my doctor strongly recommended medication, I politely refused until I could refuse no more.

The way my doctor described the value of these drugs helped me to accept their role in my life. He said, "Imagine you and I were standing in a room with broken glass littering the entire floor, and our job was to pick up all the many shards of glass. We could do it, but we'd have to move slowly and carefully to avoid cutting our hands while we went about our work. Now imagine that we had been given work gloves to help accomplish the same task. How much easier would our work be and how much faster would we get it done if we put on the gloves? Think of these meds as work gloves that you need for a time while you do some work. They'll help you get into the work faster and protect you from some of the sharper edges. Then when you're finished, you can take them off. Or leave them on. The choice will be yours. Accepting a drug today does not mean you have to accept it forever."

That did it for me.

I started taking the drugs.

Guess what? They helped. A lot.

That's not to say the decision was easy. For a long time after the drugs started helping with my anxiety and depression, I continued to feel shame about taking them. I told no one other than my wife, and even then I tried to avoid taking the pill in front of her. I was desperately worried that if people found out their pastor needed an antidepressant, they wouldn't respect me as a leader.

I remember once seeing a well-known Christian leader post a photo of his medicine bottle (which happened to be the exact same drug and dose I take) to social media and thinking that was a bad idea because people would naturally think less of him for it. Clearly, I had some internal conflict and shame around this issue. For years I kept my antidepressant in my closet next to my socks, which, if you're wondering, is not where the other medication in the household is stored. I'll never forget the day I went to get the little pill and made the decision to take the bottle out of the closet and place it alongside the other medication in my medicine cabinet. *I am no longer ashamed of taking this*, I thought. *So why am I acting as if I am?*

That was a big day for me because it meant I had fully begun to accept the reality of the medication's necessity in my life. God comes to us all in so many ways. One of the ways he comes to me and cares for me is through a tiny pill I take every morning. After I moved the pill bottle into the cabinet, I found myself more easily able to share this aspect of my life with others, which felt good because it was honest and true.

Learning to accept and love the parts of ourselves we'd rather keep in the dark is one of the most empowering experiences in life. God loves every part of us. We should too! I take medication. It's part of who I am. I can beat myself up about it or trust that I am exactly the person God made me to be. I've tried denial. Self-acceptance is a lot more fun.

Mental health medication can be a confusing and touchy subject for many Christians, something I understand deeply. But because these medications are vital in the lives of many who suffer from mental illness, and because there is often a bias against using them in Christian communities, I want to take some time to discuss them further.

One of the best perspectives I've come across when it comes to Christians and mental health medications is the one provided by Dr. Warren Kinghorn of Duke University. Kinghorn is a great example of a psychiatrist who uses his Christian faith to inform how he practices medicine. He is not only interested in healing broken bodies but tending to the embodied souls of his patients as well.

In an article for *Church Health Reader*, Kinghorn wrote about a conversation he had with a man who was fighting to come out of a dark spell of depression, one that had lasted several years, robbing him of precious time with his young children. With the help of medication, talk therapy, and electroconvulsive therapy (ECT),[1] he was starting to get better. Still, the man was nervous that the depression might once again return or the meds would stop working. Kinghorn

---

1 ECT is not a treatment of torture as it is so often portrayed in the media. In fact, it is one of the safest and most effective treatments available for depression. With ECT, electrodes are placed on the patient's scalp and a finely controlled electric current is applied while the patient is under general anesthesia. These currents cause a brief seizure that "resets" the brain, often relieving symptoms of severe depression. ECT is not normally employed until a patient has proven to be severely resistant to other forms of medication and therapy. Although ECT has been around since the 1940s and '50s, the procedure is still greatly misunderstood by the general public.

responded, "I can't promise that you won't ever be depressed again, or that we won't need to alter your current treatment. . . . But I can promise that no matter what, I'll walk with you."[1] And with those words, doctor and patient agreed to walk forward together no matter what lay ahead.

How beautiful is that?

Kinghorn wrote that "walking together is the guiding metaphor" for his work as a psychiatrist and central to his understanding of the Christian faith, drawing on the psalmist who wrote, "Blessed are those . . . whose hearts are set on pilgrimage" (Ps. 84:5). In this life, we are either moving toward God or falling away, thus Saint Thomas Aquinas's imagery of the Christian as a wayfarer or traveler on a great journey.[2] Within this theological framework, the primary question when it comes to choosing treatments for mental health patients is, "What is needed right now for the journey?"[3] Depending on the stage of the journey, patients might need medication or a support group or a simple change in sleeping habits. It all depends on where they happen to be.

That means we can't be closed off to the possibility that, at some stage, medication may be needed. Some psychiatric difficulties represent the power that nature has over our lives. When a brain disorder interrupts a person's ability to manage mood, memory, language, or perception, drugs are necessary; these are biological conditions that need pharmacological interventions. Conversely, some psychiatric disorders are a result of stress or distorted thinking processes, and medication is not always necessary for treatment. Often, psychotherapy alone can be effective in bringing about healing in these situations. The question of whether or not medication is needed must be made on a case-by-case basis, just as it is with any other medical malady.

Despite the efficacy of the mental health drugs available today, it's been my experience that many Christians either downright denounce their usage or feel great shame about taking them. Some of the reasons Christians do so are well grounded, and I completely understand them. If there is a natural treatment or a change in diet or exercise that could bring about the same sought-after improvement, then that is the course of action a lot of people would rather take. I totally get that and, in fact, recommend it myself. In general, when it comes to putting drugs in our bodies, less is almost always more. That said, let's further discuss when mental health medications are not only helpful but also necessary.

WHEN SHOULD WE TURN TO DRUGS?

Even though mental health medications have helped me tremendously, I don't want to imply, on any level, that they are the be-all and end-all when it comes to mental illness. They're not. If you're suffering from depression as the result of an abusive relationship, there isn't an antidepressant in the world that's going to solve that problem. What you need is to safely leave the relationship and surround yourself with people who love and cherish you and are willing to protect you.

Likewise, if you're experiencing debilitating shame from excessive consumption of pornography, what you need is a form of behavior modification therapy to help you change your pattern of behavior. Mental health issues are complicated, and there is no magic pill that will cure each and every disorder or problematic situation.

That said, there are certain conditions for which medication can be very helpful when appropriately prescribed and monitored by a trained physician, preferably a psychiatrist who has spent years learning about not only the body but also the mind and the complexity of human behavior. Let's go back to Kinghorn, who is exactly that, for three scenarios where it appears *obviously* good for a Christian to use a mental health medication:[4]

1. When there is evidence that the body is not supporting a person's ability to think, feel, or act appropriately in a given situation.

Think here of a situation where a person is hallucinating, literally hearing voices and seeing shapes and figures that do not actually exist. These symptoms often occur in patients battling schizophrenia. For the person with this illness, the voices are every bit as real as anything else. Clearly, in this situation, the brain needs some help to effectively do its job. Or, think of patients suffering from bipolar disorder, who experience manic phases where their energy jumps through the roof and sometimes go for days without sleep, all the while engaging in risky behavior like sex with strangers or splurging on shopping sprees. These are situations where an illness clearly inhibits a person's ability to choose wise actions, and thus medication is an appropriate form of treatment to reduce the problematic symptoms. To deny a patient medication in these scenarios would be just as wrong as keeping insulin from a diabetic.

2. When a person's suffering is so extreme it has no practical moral value.

Suffering, while not inherently good, can from time to time produce positive effects in our lives by strengthening our resolves and granting us a newfound perspective. Moreover, suffering is not a condition that can be avoided in this life. With respect to mental health, we all suffer to some degree with sadness or garden-variety anxiety. Many of us will even experience sadness that meets the criteria for clinical depression. For those who do, if tended to appropriately, depression is a highly treatable condition.

When mental illness is severe enough, however, the pain can cross the line from tolerable to intolerable. For a person who has not experienced the more intense suffering of mental illness, this can be a difficult concept to explain. In his brilliant book, *Darkness Visible*, William Styron offered a glimpse into this deeper form of suffering. He wrote:

> The pain is unrelenting, and what makes the condition intolerable is the foreknowledge that no remedy will come—not in a day, an hour, a month, or a minute. If there is mild relief, one knows that it is only temporary; more pain will follow. It is hopelessness even more than pain that crushes the soul. So the decision-making of daily life involves not, as in normal affairs, shifting from one annoying situation to another less annoying—or from discomfort to relative comfort, or from boredom to activity—but moving from pain to pain. One does not abandon, even briefly, one's bed of nails, but is attached to it wherever one goes.[5]

For some, the pain of depression can be so heavy that it all but paralyzes their lives. In these situations, like the one Styron described, medication is needed to reduce the intensity of suffering so they can have more space to act.

On a related note, medications are absolutely necessary for people who enter psychotic states and become dangerous to themselves or to others. To deny a mental health medication to a person suffering psychosis seems not only cruel but also fundamentally non-Christian.

3. When medication can help a person develop a healthier pattern of response.

When it comes to addiction there are certain mental health medications that are highly useful in helping patients stop using their drug of choice. Naltrexone, for example, blocks heroin's ability to make a person feel high. Consequently, a person who is addicted to heroin can be greatly aided by taking naltrexone because it blunts the effect of the desired drug, making it easier for the patient to learn a healthier coping mechanism instead. Moreover, a drug like methadone can actually block a person's cravings for opioids altogether, making the task of recovery vastly safer.

WHEN CAN MENTAL HEALTH MEDICATIONS BE DETRIMENTAL?

Mental health medications do not work as cures for mental illness but are effective symptom reducers. Consequently, it's imperative that we conceive of these drugs as only one aspect of treating mental illness. Otherwise, we are in danger of falling into a purely biological approach to mental health.

As has been stated again and again in this book, there is always more going on with a person than biology. For total health and an appropriate Christian perspective, the soul must be treated along with the body. So, if medications reduce symptoms in ways that blunt our emotional and intellectual responses, we need to be wary of them. Their ultimate purpose should be to remove any obstacles keeping us from moving closer to God and living his abundant life, not to lessen our ability to do so. In other words, we don't want people medicated to the point where they effectively can do nothing except sit around all day in a semicatatonic state.

WHAT SHOULD WE KNOW ABOUT SPECIFIC MENTAL HEALTH MEDICATIONS?

Mental health medications are not homogenous. Antidepressants are different from benzodiazepines, which are different from beta-blockers, which are different from mood stabilizers, and so on. I cannot, in a few short pages, give a comprehensive overview of all mental health medications, nor am I qualified to do so. What I can do, however, is offer a short description of some of the most commonly prescribed drugs: antidepressants.

Antidepressants are drugs that fight back against depression and anxiety. When a person experiences depression, this often means certain chemicals (neurotransmitters) have dropped below an optimal level. Antidepressants work to raise these neurotransmitters back to their normal levels, which relieves some of the symptoms of depression. Antidepressants can also be effective in relieving symptoms of anxiety and thus are often prescribed for patients with anxiety disorders.

When considering antidepressants, doctors are primarily looking for sustained physiological symptoms. The following list includes some of the more common physiological symptoms that could indicate a potential biochemical function:

- Sleep disturbance (this can include waking up too early in the morning, inefficient sleep, multiple awakenings during the night, or too much sleep)

- Change in appetite (this can include increased or decreased appetite that includes a change in weight)
- Fatigue
- Inflammation
- Decreased sex drive
- Restlessness or agitation
- Lower mood in the morning
- Inability to concentrate
- Decreased memory
- Loss of ability to experience pleasure

The most common complaint about antidepressants is that they do not work fast enough. On average, antidepressants take four to six weeks to reach peak effectiveness. Some patients, however, report feeling positive effects in as soon as ten days to two weeks. In many patients, it should be noted, antidepressants initially cause an increase in symptoms before a reduction. This can make the first few days or weeks on an antidepressant a bumpy ride. Sometimes a psychiatrist might prescribe another medication, such as a benzodiazepine or a beta-blocker, to help with the transition. The most important thing to remember is to continue taking the medication as prescribed by the doctor. Do not take more or less than prescribed without speaking with your doctor about doing so.

The other common complaint about antidepressants is the unpleasant side effects experienced by some patients. The side effects are wide-ranging, depending on the prescribed drug. The following list includes some of the more frequently cited negative side effects. It should be noted that many are lessened over time.

- Nausea
- Fatigue
- Insomnia
- Dry mouth
- Dizziness
- Constipation
- Sexual side effects

When experiencing unwanted side effects caused by antidepressants, though, never abruptly stop taking them, as doing so may cause extremely uncomfortable symptoms of withdrawal.

Frequently Asked Questions About Antidepressants

Most patients have more questions about antidepressants than about other types of medications doctors might prescribe. Because, unlike a steroid shot for inflammation or an antibiotic for a bug, taking an antidepressant carries more baggage. It feels more like a permanent decision that somehow affects our identity. Whether that is true, of course, depends on individual patients and how they choose to perceive the decision to accept or not accept the life-giving power these drugs can have. Either way, feeling inquisitive about these medications is common. Below I've collected some of the more common questions and tried to offer short, helpful replies.

Will an antidepressant get me high?

No. In fact, for most patients, taking the pill produces no feelings at all for at least a few days until the drug begins to build up in a person's system. When it does, the feeling experienced is not a buzz or a high but hopefully merely an absence of the troubling symptoms.

Will an antidepressant make me sad?

Maybe. Some patients report perceiving their feelings more intensely at the onset of antidepressant treatment. Some, however, report that their feelings have been muted. The thing to remember is that an antidepressant will not prevent you from being sad in the same way it will also not prevent you from being happy. People taking anti-depressants are able to experience the full range of natural human emotions.

Will an antidepressant make me act like a different person?

Depression and anxiety often make people behave in ways that are different from their normal personality. Most mental health professionals agree that personality is a long-standing set of char-acteristics that emerge sometime during childhood and typically persist throughout life. But depression often makes people feel like their personality has been stolen away. What antidepressants are likely to do is help you feel more like yourself before the depression set in as opposed to a new person altogether.

If one antidepressant does not appear to be working, should I try another one?

Due to the complexities of these drugs and the different ways they affect people, patients often have to try one or two to get the right fit. This trial-and-error process is one of the many reasons why I recommend seeing a psychiatrist and not just a general practitioner for prescribing and managing mental health medications. Fortunately, doctors can now run a quick DNA test that helps identify which drugs your body does or does not metabolize well. In a study presented at the American Psychiatric Association annual meeting in 2018, researchers reported that people using genetic testing

(GeneSight) were 50 percent more likely to experience a remission in their symptoms after eight weeks of treatment compared with patients not using the test.[6] What these tests can't do is identify which antidepressant will be most effective for any individual, but they are enormously helpful in identifying which drugs ought to be avoided. This can make the whole process of trying antidepressants far less traumatic and far more efficient.

Can antidepressants make you suicidal?

No. The reason people often mistakenly believe this is that a suicidal person often becomes more suicidal when coming out of a depression. There are various reasons for this, with one of the most important being that often a suicidal person who is extremely depressed wants to die but simply does not have the energy to do so. However, in the early stages of a depression lifting, energy returns but the psychological problems still exist, creating a potentially dangerous situation.

MEDICATION AS A GIFT

I can divide my life into two halves: living with anxiety on my own and then living with anxiety with the help of a skilled therapist *and* medication. You have to understand, after accepting the Lord Jesus Christ as my Savior and marrying my wife, it's the third most important decision I've ever made. I have no problem admitting the work I do now is only made possible because of medication. Call it a crutch. Call it a weakness. I don't care. I call it my reality. And my reality is one I enjoy much more than the previous one where I denied myself the fruit of one of God's greatest gifts: medicine.

TWELVE

PEOPLE

Before I went away for in-patient treatment, I called a good friend to tell him that I showed up drunk for work. I'll never forget what he said back to me.

"The best people I know go to rehab."

I can't even begin to tell you what that kind of acceptance did for me. In a moment when I felt completely abnormal, he normalized the situation for me. Just knowing he had other friends who had found themselves in similar situations immediately made me feel like less of a freak. Not only that, he was sincerely telling me that the "best people" he knew were the ones who went to rehab. What did that even mean? I didn't know then (although I suspect I do now), but *holy cow* it felt good to hear because it gave me hope. Maybe this wasn't the end of my life after all? Nothing about going to rehab was easy, but that little conversation did me a world of good as I tried to steady my heart and mind for what lay ahead.

I'm convinced that if more people knew they'd get the kind of support my friend offered me, the number of people who actually seek help would skyrocket. Which, by the way, is something we desperately need, since less than 10 percent of people who struggle with any form of substance use disorder ever seek professional help.[1] *Less than 10 percent.* Let it melt your brain.

Of the 10 percent who actually do seek help, how many do you think find lasting sobriety in recovery? If we use the most optimistic numbers out there, it's maybe 15 percent. If you're doing the math, that means—*at best*—only 1.5 percent of Americans whose lives are currently being ruined by booze and opioids and the rest of the intoxicant gang ever find freedom from it.

Why?

Because far too many people don't have intimate relationships with people they can genuinely trust. It's pretty neat that I can Tweet to somebody in Japan whom I'll never meet in person, but I'd much rather know the names of my next-door neighbors any day. And the truth is, I don't. We live in the most connected *and* isolated world in the history of humanity. I can't be the only one who vacillates between obsessing over the next iPhone and seriously wishing the thing had never been invented in the first place.

There's this incredible episode on Amazon Prime Video's show *Modern Love* where Anne Hathaway plays a character with bipolar disorder. I don't want to ruin the episode for you (because it's seriously that good), but near the end of the show her character decides to reveal the truth of her condition for the first time in her life. Up until this point she has been convinced that, if anyone knew about her illness, she'd be rejected outright. In a moment of courage, she tells a former colleague the truth. Instead of shunning Hathaway's character, the colleague chooses instead to lean into the friendship. This simple act of leaning in works a miracle in the life of Hathaway's character. Armed with the knowledge that she is loved just as she is—illness and all—a new life of healing becomes available to her.[2]

Jesus took leaning in to other people to a whole new level. Think back to the earliest days of his ministry. After he was baptized by John the Baptist and spent forty days fasting and praying, he set about his public ministry and immediately began collecting disciples. It's easy to focus on the significance of this for the disciples. Jesus picked them to be the disciples! That's a big deal. But flip the script for a moment and consider the impact on Jesus. I think Jesus needed the disciples as much as the disciples needed him.

Jesus understood that he was going to need the love and support that can only be found in close relationship with trustworthy people. Jesus was a human, which meant he needed other humans. If Jesus Christ needed close relationships in order to live his best life, then surely we do too. Unfortunately, when mental illness strikes, we often want to withdraw from those we love. We must resist the temptation to isolate at every possible turn. Battling mental illness is tough enough on its own. Doing it alone is darn near impossible.

The truth is that we have to find our people for at least the following four reasons:

OXYTOCIN

Oxytocin is a little chemical in the brain that makes us feel good when we connect, in person, with other living beings. You know how good it feels when you hug a friend you haven't seen in a long time? That's oxytocin doing its job. The more oxytocin our brains release the more social we become.

Studies have shown that oxytocin encourages us to be more open and generous to other people. It also helps us trust others more. This is important because mental illness often keeps us from wanting to socialize with others. If we give in to the isolation, we deny ourselves opportunities for more oxytocin, which then further inhibits our desire to connect. But if we can get out and go to that support group, meet up with that friend, or attend that church service, our brains will literally be in a better condition to do it again the next time.

Oxytocin is an enormously important chemical in the fight against depression and anxiety. The good news is that it's readily available, as near as the closest friend.

BELONGING

There are few worse feelings than believing you don't fit in to a group. Your accent is wrong. You don't have on the right shoes. You didn't grow up in the posh neighborhood. Whatever it is that makes you different gets magnified with mental illness, and, before you know it, you're not just different from everyone else—you're an alien.

I will never forget the immense loneliness I felt during my first days of college. I had enrolled at a large private university on the West Coast where I literally did not know a soul. Until then I didn't know it was possible to be around thousands of people but feel infinitely lonely.

We can feel lonely around others because it's not the proximity to bodies that we need but the sense of belonging to the other bodies that matters most. We need to know and be known. This happens when a group accepts us for who we are, not the person we can contort ourselves into being to earn belonging.

When it comes to mental health, having a place of belonging is crucial, especially during periods of isolation or self-loathing. To know you have people who will receive you without judgment can be a godsend. This is why support groups and recovery groups do so much good work. Unlike a team or a business or a church where you often have to perform or maintain a certain image to belong, groups designed to support mental health focus on welcoming and lifting up exactly those who might have faced exclusion elsewhere. I can't help but think of Jesus' example of eating and drinking with "notorious sinners." He understood how valuable a simple invitation to the table is.

SUPPORT

Nobody makes it through this life alone. Regardless of how successful or powerful we are, there will come a day when we need support from someone else. My father once had to pick me up off the floor of my bedroom closet and carry me to bed because I was so overwhelmed with anxiety. I was a thirty-five-year-old man when that happened. Not only that, my father would have never been there had my wife not picked up the phone to call him and say we needed help. Where would I be today without the people in my life who have committed to supporting me? I shudder at the thought.

I'm lucky because I have family who support me, but I understand many don't. Anytime I bring up this issue of support, someone always tells me afterward that they don't have friends and have run out of options for trying to find them. I have no easy answer to that problem. What I say, though, is that you have to keep chasing a group who will support you in troubling times, like a man dying of thirst in the desert. Because it's not a matter of if you'll get thirsty but when.

God did not create us to live our lives in isolation. We need one another. And it's up to us to find one another so that when the crisis comes, we can also be found.

The image I keep in my mind is the one of the paralytic Mark told us about in his gospel, whose friends brought him to Jesus on a mat. When they arrived, the house was so full they couldn't get inside, so they climbed on top of the house, cut out a hole, and lowered their friend down to be healed (2:3–4). Those are real friends. The kind of people who don't just show up for the good times but who are willing to stick around when the going gets rough and do whatever it takes to make sure you're okay. Find your people. Force yourself to do it. They just might save your life.

PURPOSE

If you ever get involved in the AA community, or others like it, you'll discover one of the primary ways folks stay sober is by keeping a high level of commitment to helping others. When cravings for alcohol set in or symptoms of depression reappear, one of the best ways to divert the brain into a more positive thought pattern is to focus on the needs of another person. Helping will almost always distract a person long enough to allow the cravings to pass. Not only does it break a negative pattern of thought, it also leaves a person feeling good about having done something for someone else. Not to mention the fact that somebody else gets helped out in the process!

STRATEGIES FOR AVOIDING ISOLATION

I once had to preach a sermon about the importance of tithing at a time when I wasn't tithing properly myself. Standing in front of a congregation and talking about something I myself wasn't willing to do was the epitome of a hypocritical experience. I felt awful. I tell you that because what I'm about to recommend to you in this section about avoiding isolation are all things I find very hard to do. When I'm depressed or drinking too much, I avoid intimate connection with other people like the plague. But I'm telling you, when I don't do that and allow myself to be touched and loved on by other people, everything gets better. So even though I don't always take this medicine myself, I'm going to shove it down your throat anyway. Like I said, I'm a hypocrite. Deal with it.

1. **Call a friend you haven't seen in a while or who lives far away.** When you're struggling, it can feel anxiety-provoking to talk to a friend you see regularly who might already suspect something is going on with you. That person might ask you what is wrong, and maybe you're not ready to talk about that. So talk to that out-of-town friend; everyone appreciates a call to catch up. Ask lots of questions, and allow yourself to get lost in the stories of your friend's life. When the friend asks you how you're doing, you can keep it brief (you don't have to divulge what's going on with you) and say you've just been realizing how important it is to remain connected with the people you care about. This will allow you to have a conversation with a friend that will keep you from feeling as lonely, but do so in a way that will prevent you from having to be more vulnerable than you're prepared to be.

2. **Make use of text messages.** While we all know texting does not allow for the same level of intimacy as a voice conversation, it can be the perfect form of communication when you're tempted to isolate. Keep texting and responding to text messages you receive. It's far better than nothing.

3. **Go for walks in your neighborhood and force yourself to wave and smile at the people you see.** This kind of contact hardly ever leads to invasive conversation. But the simple acknowledgement of other people and their acknowledgement of you will feel good and remind you that even though you don't feel like connecting deeply with people now, you will someday soon.

4. **Avoid using delivery apps for food.** This one isn't as applicable since the start of the pandemic. Using apps and avoiding the grocery store is, in some cases, what must be done for safety. That said, when possible, getting out of the house for food is an easy way to interact with people, even if they are strangers and the interaction is transactional in nature. You never know who may pay you a nice compliment on your hair or your outfit. The potential for a tiny conversation that could spark something positive in your mind is always there if you're out and about. But if you stay in, there is absolutely no chance this can happen.

5. **Use social media.** It often gets a bad rap, and for good reason, but the ability to virtually connect with others can be a godsend when depressed. The little touches you can get from a comment here or a comment there also keep you connected in ways that will remind you that you'll want to return to a more robust social life in the future.

6. **Finally, if you can manage it, confide in a friend that you are isolating and give that friend permission to check on you and invite you to do things.** Explain that you're really struggling and not up for much, but that you know you need some social contact. A trusted friend who is willing to have a quiet cup of coffee or go for a walk can serve as a lifeline until you're ready to dive back in. The main thing to remember is:

Do not cut yourself off completely. Why? Because there was only one thing God said wasn't good. And by this point in the book you know exactly what that is.

FRIENDS SHOW US WHAT'S POSSIBLE

A few years ago, I was sitting in my favorite coffee shop trying to put words on a blank screen when the name of an old college buddy appeared on my phone. We hadn't spoken in a few months, and so I was surprised when he skipped the pleasantries to ask me if I had recently spoken to another friend of ours who had been in the news. And by news, I mean one of the biggest media frenzies in the history of media frenzies. That's what happens when you make the most viral video in the history of the internet.

Wade asked, "Have you talked to Jason today? Or in the past few days?"

"We've texted," I said, "but, obviously, you know, he's pretty busy right now."

"Are you online right now?"

"Yeah," I said. "I'm working."

"TMZ is saying he was just arrested for masturbating in public."

I punched *TMZ* into my search engine.

Jason was my big brother in our fraternity in college. I adored him and basically wanted to be him in college. I *still* kind of want to be Jason. I think most people who know him feel that way. He's just a special kind of guy who defies every notion of the word *typical*. He has energy unlike anyone else I've ever known and a curiosity for life that would impress Benjamin Franklin. And his heart. His heart is as vast as the Pacific Ocean he loves to surf.

I'll put it this way. There was a large homeless population around the edges of our college campus in South Los Angeles. I walked past these people every day without, shamefully, giving them much thought, as did most of my peers. Jason, on the other hand, knew their names, took them to buy groceries, and sat beside them for hours, collecting the intimate details of their lives. He knew them, and they knew him. You've heard of people who have never met a stranger. Well, until I met Jason, I didn't know there were also people who had never met a stranger they didn't love. That's just who Jason is. He is filled with love. He also has a wicked thirst for adventure, a thirst that sent him and two other friends to film a documentary about the war in Darfur.

While there, Jason and his team witnessed some horrific violence against children that led them on a journey where they began to learn about a man named Joseph Kony and the Lord's Resistance Army. Sensing an important story, Jason and the team shifted the focus of their film to the civil war in Uganda. Subsequently, they made a documentary about the atrocities in Uganda and founded a nonprofit called Invisible Children that hoped to bring Joseph Kony to justice and rescue some of the untold number of children who'd been drafted into his guerrilla armies.

Jason first traveled to Uganda in 2003. When Wade called me that day in the coffee shop, it was 2012, and Invisible Children had set the internet ablaze with its newest documentary, *Kony 2012*. Within hours of the video going live on YouTube, it had thousands of views. Then it was tens of thousands of views, followed by hundreds of thousands, which led to one million views. And the party was just getting started. Within days it had become the most viral video in the history of the internet, eventually amassing more than a hundred million views.

Overnight Jason went from little-known filmmaker to world-wide media celebrity, giving interviews to everyone from Larry King to Oprah. And then, of course, there was a *TIME* magazine cover. Yeah, he was on the cover of *TIME*.

At first it all seemed great. The plight Jason and his crew at Invisible Children had been working to reveal was finally given the attention it richly deserved. Maybe now something could be done to protect those poor children whose lives were being destroyed. But not everyone was pleased with the work of Invisible Children. Given their meteoric rise, an enormous amount of criticism followed suit. Which, to some degree, could be expected. But then something very unexpected happened.

Jason got sick.

In public.

When I got on *TMZ* like Wade told me to, I saw a cell phone video showing Jason naked in public, ranting to himself about evil, slapping the pavement, and generally showing signs of a person in severe mental distress. There was nothing funny about it, but *TMZ* and the rest of the internet seemed to find it hilarious. For the next twenty-four hours I lived on the internet while social media tore my friend apart, criticizing everything from the way he walked and talked to his efforts at freeing children from slavery in Africa.

Jason remembers almost nothing of what happened because he was having a psychotic break, something that can happen to anyone should they experience enough stress. He wasn't drunk. He wasn't on drugs. He was a person experiencing an acute mental health struggle. And the internet was merciless about it.

Here's my question. If Jason had suffered a seizure in public, do you think he'd have been ridiculed as he was? What about a stroke or a heart attack?

No way. Why not? We don't find those kinds of medical conditions funny because we understand how serious they are. We get the fact that they are life-threatening and beyond a person's control. But because mental health conditions express themselves in ways that appear volitional, odd, and extreme, we feel the freedom to attack individuals for their behavior. It's cruel, ignorant, and insanely dangerous.

The internet said he masturbated in public.

No one at the scene actually reported that happened.

The internet said he was arrested.

Actually, the police didn't arrest him. They did an excellent job at recognizing they weren't dealing with a criminal but a person having a mental health crisis who needed assistance. Which is why they took him to a hospital and not a jail.

Where he stayed for a while.

And guess what?

He got better.

Not in a few hours.

Not in a few days.

Not in a few weeks.

But he got better, much better, over time.

He didn't quit. And I, for one, am especially glad he didn't. Do you remember the friend who told me the best people he knows go to rehab? The one who lifted my spirit when I was dangerously close to bottoming out? The one who didn't judge me for one second because he spoke the language of my pain?

It was the same friend who braved the epic comeback I just told you about.

People. Get. Better.

And when they do, they're often the best ones to help others who need to get better.

We can't be alone. We have to get out there and connect with other people who understand the pain of mental illness and are journeying through their own recoveries because the truth is, a lot of people won't ever be able to fully understand what we are going through. And that's okay. We can't expect every person to become an expert in how to be sensitive and caring when it comes to issues of mental health. This makes it all the more important for us to ensure, however, that there are people in our lives who do.

Please don't underestimate the power of connecting with other people when it comes to mental health. And don't just take my word for it, but remember God himself told us this truth in the first pages of Genesis. It's not now, nor has it ever been, good for us to be alone.

THIRTEEN

PUTTING TREATMENT
ALL TOGETHER

Here's what depression looks like for me:

- I cancel plans with friends at the last moment.
- My anxiety is out of control, usually spiking in the morning when I wake up.
- I suffer panic attacks.
- I stop reading books and instead mindlessly surf the internet.
- I spend money I don't have.
- Playing with my children feels like a burden instead of the most fun thing in the world, which is how I feel about it when I'm well.
- I'm not very interested in having sex. Sometimes I try and am not even able to do it.
- I don't care about watching sports.
- My prayer life dries up fast because I have nothing to say to God and feel like he has nothing to say to me.

- I lie about how bad I'm feeling. This lying makes me feel even worse.
- My favorite time of day becomes the three in the morning wake-up because I know I still have three hours before I'll be forced out of bed and back into real life.
- I stop exercising. The mere thought of it feels impossible.
- My appetite plummets.
- I feel dizzy, and my limbs feel hollow.
- I struggle to make small talk at parties because I'm convinced nobody wants to hear anything I have to say.
- I crave alcohol in ways I know are unhealthy. I don't want to drink with friends. I want instead to drink alone because I want the alcohol for one purpose only: to numb my feelings.
- I worry constantly that my children will learn the truth about me and wish they had a different father.
- I worry my wife wishes she would have married someone who doesn't struggle with depression.

Talk therapy, medication, and other people are the three legs of my stool for treating mental illness. I need them all, and I use them all. But if I don't first know what depression looks like for me, and what I need in response to that, then I won't be able to make the most of my treatment to combat my struggles more specifically. The same will go for you.

So, as we are winding down our conversation about the treatments and tools we can employ toward mental health, let's zero in on how to make sure your specific needs are being taken care of. To do this, you'll need to check in with your biopsychosocial-spiritual self, carefully looking at each dimension of your existence. Here's how I do it. I call it my comprehensive mental scan.

BIOLOGY

To start, I look at the physical dimensions of my life, paying special attention to the areas where I have struggled in the past and am most likely to struggle in the future. That way I'm tailoring my treatments for what I specifically need.

For example, I take meds. I've got to do it, and I'm not ashamed of it. I used to be, but not anymore. My body needs a pill to function properly. It's as simple as that. So I need to take my meds faithfully. A common problem for those of us who struggle is that we can be inconsistent with taking our medication. Some of us simply forget, while others of us resist our medication in either conscious or unconscious protests of denial. If we don't take our meds and we can function, then maybe we aren't as sick as we thought we were? Here's the deal: if we've been prescribed any kind of mental health medication by a physician, then we need to take those meds as prescribed unless otherwise directed by the professionals we have entrusted ourselves to.

What about booze? As you already know, I went through a period of life where I abused alcohol. I never got to the point where I needed alcohol to function. I didn't drink in the morning. I didn't get the shakes if I went without. What I did was prioritize it as my number-one coping mechanism.

Feeling stressed? Have a beer. Need a creative thought? Have a beer. Hard day at work? Have a beer. Kids were hard to put to bed? Have a beer. The problem with doing this for so long is that my other skills for coping with stress began to atrophy like muscles that aren't used. In order to regain use of these muscles, I had to cut out alcohol from my life for a very long time. As Brad Pitt recently said about himself, "I removed my drinking privileges."[1]

At first this was hard and scary, but after a time, I realized I didn't need alcohol in my life. But to come to this realization, I had to practice abstinence, attend recovery meetings, and go to a lot of individual therapy. These days, while not totally abstinent, I am basically a non-drinker because my life is simply richer and less problematic without alcohol in it.

Might there be a day when I drink more? Perhaps. But I'm not worried about that now. Right now, I am caring for my body to the best of my ability in order to support my mental health, and alcohol gets in the way of me doing that. Do I miss the occasional IPA? You bet I do. Am I sometimes jealous of those who seem to have no trouble with their consumption? Yes, I am. But is that IPA worth not becoming the absolute best version of myself I can be for my wife and children? No freaking way. I've been there, and I've done that. Besides, I don't miss hangovers, and I like being able to eat that extra bar of chocolate since I'm not wasting so many calories on alcohol.

Bottom line: when I check in with myself physically, I definitely assess where I am in terms of alcohol consumption and how I'm thinking about it.

What about exercise? I have been running nearly every day since I was eighteen. I don't do it for my body, which there isn't much to speak of anyway. I do it for my brain. There is literally no better medicine for depression than exercise. If I suddenly notice that I have no desire to run or am low on energy, I know something is up and I need to pay closer attention to what is going on with me.

Paying attention to our bodies and being honest about how we physically feel is one of the best ways we can be proactive with depression and other mental illnesses.

PSYCHOLOGY

Next, I find it invaluable to do an assessment of my thought life and how I'm doing when it comes to my mind.

A large part of my psychological struggles came about because I allowed myself to become psychologically disintegrated. What do I mean by that? My mind and actions were not aligned. If my belief system is in conflict with how I live my life, I'm in trouble.

I'll save you the details, but, basically, I thought I could grin and bear a particular professional situation by keeping my genuine beliefs to myself and suffering through it. I thought I was far tougher psychologically than I am. Turns out I'm pretty fragile. I cannot pretend to be something I'm not. I am who I am. I know that now. I can live into that truth. But not doing it almost destroyed me. So I'd encourage you to pursue psychological integration. What we think and whether our actions align with those thoughts is vital. Put simply, we need to live out our deeply held values. Otherwise, things get wonky.

Also, I go to therapy and support groups. So, as part of my comprehensive mental scan, I ask myself, *Have I been attending regularly, or have I gotten lazy?* These sessions are not optional for me; they are crucial to my living a healthy life. I need to check in regularly to make sure I'm in a good place with these sessions that keep my thought life on track.

Paying attention to how we're doing psychologically is critical, and a big part of that is each one of us discovering what we need to do to keep our thought life as healthy as possible and then making sure we're keeping up with those things.

SOCIAL

We are all social beings, as we've already established. Being in healthy relationships is key to maintaining our mental health, and so another good part of the check-in process is to see how we're doing socially.

One of the great joys of the pastoral life is getting to connect with a lot of people. I am so grateful for the many connections and relationships my time in the ministry afforded me. But I woke up one day and had trouble remembering the last time I had a conversation with someone who didn't have an agenda with me. My friends were gone, and it wasn't because they abandoned me—I had abandoned them. I was so caught up in what I was doing that I didn't have time to cultivate friendships. I made that decision. And it was not good for me.

These days I pursue friendship like the living fountain it is. You gotta have your people. And finding them might be hard. But my advice is the same as earlier. Do it anyway. Having people, even if it's just one or two, you can go to—no matter what—is more valuable than anything in this world.

A few kinds of friends you need to have:

- Someone who has been given permission from you to ask hard questions. Let them ask you the questions, and then answer honestly. It's the only way this relationship can be helpful.
- Someone who is older than you who has something you want. Chase after them. Ask them questions. Find out how they got the life they have, and then do the same.
- Someone with whom you feel safe to confide in about the darker corners of your heart. Confess what you are afraid of and allow their love for you to help you love yourself.

- Someone who makes you laugh. Because we all need to laugh wildly every now and again.

Keep in mind that when Jesus gathered his band together, he didn't grab just one or two friends. He took at least twelve. I think that can be a good rule of life for all of us. Do you have at least twelve people in your life whom you can trust and call upon during times of need? If not, go find them.

SPIRITUAL

Finally, we must tend to our spirituality on a regular basis to stay mentally healthy, so it's crucial to assess ourselves on a spiritual level as well.

I tend to my spirituality in healthier ways now than I used to. The great trap for religious leaders is that we start believing our own hype. My hype was that I had some wisdom, some ability to communicate, and the ability to provide a calming presence to those in crisis. All that might be true. None of it, however, can remain true if I'm not spiritually healthy. So I had to go back to the basics and put my spiritual oxygen mask on first before attempting to offer anyone anything else. For me that's a lot of silent prayer, ordering my day with God at the top, reading Scripture, and practicing presence and compassion with each and every person I meet. Had I grounded my mental health in God, I would have been far better prepared to face my depression.

Now that I know that, I can check back in with myself regularly, asking whether I've been putting those disciplines into practice or whether I've started to let them slip. We need to be honest with ourselves about these things so that we can get back on track.

EXAMINE YOUR LIFE

Mental illness looks different for everyone, so it's critical to take the common symptoms and examine your life to see how they are or are not manifesting themselves.

Don't just ask yourself whether you feel irritable. Try and look for examples of you displaying irritability.

Don't just wonder whether you've been indecisive. Really examine how you have been making decisions, and compare that to how you have historically gone about it.

It's important to put flesh to these symptoms in order to gather an accurate picture of how mental illness might be infiltrating your life. It's like that old saying: keep your friends close but your enemies closer. Remember, we must know ourselves if we are to properly care for ourselves.

*C*hecking into treatment is an odd cross between hotel and prison. You are examined by a nurse, told to blow into a breathalyzer, and made to dump out all of your neatly packed belongings on the floor while two employees rummage through them, all while someone else politely brings you a sandwich and encourages you to take part in yoga the next morning.

You sleep your first night in the medical unit so a nurse can check your blood pressure every hour. You want to feel as though the entire experience is too surreal to actually be real, but that's not how you feel at all. As you sit on that bed in the cold and sterile medical unit, reality comes crashing down upon you. You have arrived at a very low place, separated from your family, and your career and health are in jeopardy. You weep through the night. Hard, guttural groans come up from places you didn't know existed within you. It is the longest and darkest night of your life.

The next twenty-eight days are a series of highs and lows. Long days and nights of looking inward, facing yourself, and getting brutally honest in the presence of other people who are trying to do the same. In the beginning you feel as though you have absolutely been misplaced because you, surely, have nothing in common with the people who are now your peers. They have real issues with drugs and alcohol and mental illness. They use drugs like *heroin and cocaine. Some have attempted suicide. Several of them have been to treatment more than twenty times. One woman is there for her thirty-first stay. You are not nearly as "bad" as them. You don't belong.*

But then something happens as you listen to their stories. You hear bits of yourself in each and every one. The distinction between you and them begins to break down, and a strong affection develops between all of you in a very short period of time. Each of you has come to this place in a tremendous amount of pain, and each of you wants to get better.

Within a few days you understand that you are absolutely where you are supposed to be. You do belong in this place. God has brought you here. You have fallen hard from grace, but maybe here you are being given the chance to once more be born again.

Your days in treatment are some of the most gut wrenching and glorious of your life. You eventually come to think of each day as a good day, even though there isn't a single one you would describe as easy. Getting genuinely honest about how your primary coping mechanism for stress has become alcohol makes you feel a kind of shame you did not think possible. Feelings of abject failure and pride for what you are doing and where you are staying vacillate endlessly in your heart and soul.

You miss your family. Oh, how badly you miss them. Your two little boys have been told you are on an extended work trip to California. They don't understand why you have to be gone so long. You get to speak with them briefly some evenings, and they beg you to come home. You want to tell them that you are doing this for them, but they are too young to hear this. Someday you'll have the conversation. You'll tell them the truth about everything. Until then, you pray desperately they don't inherit the genes that make you susceptible to depression and substance use disorder. You pray they are more like their mother than you.

Because the treatment facility understands religion to be deeply important to your life, they allow you to go to a local church each Sunday a few miles down the road. Someone from the facility drives you and either sits with you in the service or waits for you outside until it is over. Your only instruction is to not take the wine at Communion.

Shucks.

You go every Sunday you're in treatment. Sitting in the pews is a powerful blessing you had nearly forgotten about. How sweet it is to sit among the faithful and join in corporate worship with no other responsibilities but to lift up your open heart to God.

One Sunday you go to church with two of your friends, including a former satanist with anti-Christian tattoos covering his body. He has recently discovered the Episcopal Church, and the two of you have spent hours in conversation about God. He is slowly beginning to wonder what it might look like to welcome God into his life. Your other friend is a nineteen-year-old transgender woman who is a lifelong believer in God. The three of you make quite the trio sitting in that little church with about forty other elderly people.

The service is beautiful and the sermon powerful. On the way out the door, you thank the pastor for his words. He *keeps ahold of your hand and says, "Yes, I noticed you nod-ding along and that you were very familiar with the liturgy, but I've never seen you here before. Are you new to town?"*

"The three of us are visiting," you say.

"Well, it was lovely to have you joining us today. Will you be in town long?"

"Uh . . . probably a month or so?" The pastor looks con-fused by your confusion as to the length of your stay. In an attempt to escape the tension, you add, "I'm actually a pastor too."

"Is that so? Are you all here on a mission trip?"

You and your friends share a look. They clearly expect you to answer. You consider lying to your fellow minister. You consider telling him a thousand different stories about how it is that you have come to his little church on a bright California morning with your lapsed-satanist buddy and your pious transgender friend. You consider just walking away. What's he going to do? Chase after you and demand an accounting of why you're here? You consider any and every option other than the one you somehow know you need to choose.

And that's when the Holy Spirit shows up in power to let you know that, if you're serious about getting well, you need to get honest with yourself and everyone else.

"Actually," you say, "the three of us are staying at the in-patient rehab up the road. We're trying to get sober."

You don't wait for his response. You throw on your sun-glasses and begin walking back to the car, a pep in your step. Your friends trail behind you, cracking up with laugh-ter. Before you know it, you're smiling wider than you have in a very, very long time.

CONCLUSION

I don't recommend showing up to church drunk. It's not a good look, especially if you're the one standing up front leading the whole thing. But that's what I did. And if I'm being honest, it's still not that easy for me to write or speak about. Even now, after majorly sobering up and going through a ton of therapy, the memory of my behavior evokes a great deal of shame in me.

An older priest once told me he was working a funeral that had to be stopped midway through because the officiating priest was so drunk he couldn't perform his ritual duties. I remember hearing that story and feeling disgust toward that priest. How could he be so irresponsible, so insensitive to the grieving family? And then, as life would have it, I basically did the same thing. It may not have been a funeral, but a Sunday evening service is a sacred event where people come to worship God, not put up with ministers who can't stand straight and read coherently from the Bible.

What explanations there are for my behavior have already been given. I have no interest in offering excuses, but I do want to tell you something. While I continue to struggle with guilt over the way I allowed my depression and misuse of alcohol to negatively influence my life and burden my family, I am also incredibly grateful for what happened to me. I am grateful because showing up to church drunk became the catalyst I needed to wake up and get real about what was happening in my life. I was sick, and I desperately needed to get well for myself, for my wife, and for the two little boys who call me Dad.

I now view these episodes with what mental health professionals like to call multiple truths. *Multiple truths* means we can feel opposite ends of the emotional spectrum at the same time without one of those feelings negating the validity of the other. I can feel sad and happy about what happened without diminishing the depth and sincerity of my experience. Does that make sense? I really hope it does. Taking this nonbinary approach to the darker seasons of our lives can be a wonderful way of moving forward and out of them. It provides access to a superpower that saved my life: gratitude.

My sudden departure and subsequent resignation from the church I served affected people I love quite negatively, and I don't want to ever make light of that. A part of me will forever wish things could have been different. Part of me will forever regret and feel sorry. I don't feel sorry for getting sick, but I do feel sorry for the ways I allowed my illness to desecrate public worship and let down the flock I'd been entrusted to lead and love.

But, as we close our time together, I also want to be radically honest in this moment because I imagine some reading this book feel the opposite of gratitude when it comes to their battles with mental health and the corresponding events of their lives. I imagine some of you believe that finding any good in your depression or anxiety is impossible.

Here's the thing: If you're reading this right now, your fight isn't over. There is still air in your lungs and hope in your future. There is nothing about your future that is set in stone except for two facts:

God loves you, and you have freedom to choose what kind of life you want to live. That's it.

I don't care how many times someone has told you that you're an addict and will never amount to anything. I don't care how many times you've told yourself you're worthless and don't deserve to live. I don't care if you've been to rehab twenty times. You are still alive, which means you can get better. And for that simple fact, the fact that it's not over yet, you can be grateful. And maybe there, in that tiniest sliver of gratitude, you can find the strength to make the next move, the move that may very well save and transform your life.

Go in peace, my dear friends, on the journey back toward God and yourself. I'll be making the same journey. At times I'll be sprinting, the wind in my hair, a smile on my face. Other nights I'll be limping along, barely putting one foot in front of the other, hoping to make it to the sunrise. There will be times I'll fall to the ground, certain I've reached the end of the line. But I am bound and determined to get back up and never give up because, by God's grace, I have made the decision to keep traveling down the good path God has given me, trusting it will someday lead me home. I hope to see you along the way. In fact, I need to see you along the way because I don't think I'll make it alone.

Peace and love, my friends. May you, too, never, ever stop walking.

A FINAL THOUGHT FOR CHRISTIANS WHO DON'T SUFFER FROM MENTAL ILLNESS

If there is one principle or maxim you take away from reading this book, I hope it's this: the single most helpful thing we Christians can do to support those of us who struggle with depression or any other kind of mental illness is to simply be honest about its existence. If we can find the courage to face the reality of what is happening, then we can trust God will lead us from there and show us how each of us can individually and specifically minister to those who need our love and support.

One of the most powerful ways we can do this is by committing to honesty about mental illness—even when it does its worst damage, as it does in suicide. There isn't a singular or simple answer as to what Christians should say or do at the funeral of someone who died by suicide, but I do believe it's imperative that we're as honest as we can be because people listen at funerals in ways they don't always listen at other times. Death, unlike religious belief, unites every single person alive. This makes funerals highly teachable and sometimes even life-saving moments. I can't tell you what should be done in every situation, but I can tell you what I did when faced with the situation.

Let me tell you about James. He was smart, charismatic, and loved by his family and friends. In many ways he had it all. James also had major depressive disorder. At our last dinner together, we discussed his pending divorce, how much he missed his children, and the complexity of living back home with his mom and dad as a thirtysomething who'd previously been a successful businessman in the high-stakes world of corporate finance. We ate good food and enjoyed each other's company. Both of us cried. We hugged. We parted with hopeful words.

I never saw him again.

A few weeks later I stood in the vaulted pulpit of a Gothic church to preach the homily at his funeral. Next to performing last rites for a newborn whom I'd baptized only hours earlier, preaching this funeral was the toughest thing I'd done as a pastor. It hit way too close to home.

Those of us who struggle with our mental health are keenly aware of how fragile our psyches are. When you've had to fight to get out of bed in the morning or tuck yourself in the fetal position to ride out a bumpy panic attack, the illusion of your own invincibility gets shot to pieces. Mental illness feeds you mouthfuls of sour grapes from the Tree of Knowledge that open your mind to the reality that madness lives far closer than you ever want to believe.

Which is scary, as the truth so often is. James's death scared me because I knew another truth about us: We were brothers in depression. That meant a simple rearranging of the facts in this story could have placed James in the pews and me in the casket as opposed to the pulpit.

But it wasn't my funeral, which meant I had a job to do. In the Anglican tradition, we believe that, while a funeral can celebrate the life of the deceased, its primary objective is to proclaim what we proclaim every Sunday, namely that Christ has died, Christ is risen, and Christ will come again. Consequently, the liturgy looks a lot like a typical Sunday morning, save for the parts where we acknowledge the dead and commend that person's spirit back to God. We don't even officially have eulogies. If they are given at all, they happen at the beginning of the service so as to not interrupt the flow of the worship. If you come from a different Christian tradition where the bulk of the funeral is dedicated to talking about the deceased, this might appear cold or insensitive. But, trust me, it is so comforting to hear the truth of the gospel proclaimed in the face of death as opposed to clunky efforts to lionize the dead.

I tell you this because we decided to do something different at James's funeral. We didn't chuck the liturgy out the window or anything, but James's father asked if I'd be willing to address the reality of mental illness in my homily. It was going to be a large funeral, and he wanted every person in the church to hear the truth about mental illness. After some serious prayer and a few sleepless nights, I took the opportunity to not only share the good news of Jesus Christ but also be honest about mental illness:

> James died from depression. He was given the best care in the world, but sometimes this is what happens. We live in a broken world where things don't always go right. You can inject the chemo, undergo the radiation, cut out the melanoma, but sometimes disease won't be stopped. So let's be honest, and helpful, and Christian. Because there are millions of others who suffer from this same disease, but they suffer in silence. James would

not want us to be silent. I knew James. I loved James. He wanted
to be well, and he would want others to be well too.

Depression is not shameful. I suffer from depression.
Depression is a reality. What we need to say today is that, like
all realities, it can be affected by God. Through God's intervention, which comes in many forms—community, friendship,
religion, therapy, medication—God heals. If you or a loved one
is struggling today, please know there is so much help, and that
you are not alone.

The response was immediate and overwhelming. Crowds of
people told me they had never heard a minister say such things in a
church. These were lawyers, judges, TV anchors, and professional
athletes, many of whom were eager to talk with me about their own
battles with depression and anxiety.

On one hand I was relieved it was over and grateful my admis-
sion might have made it easier for others to share their own. On the
other hand, I was deeply saddened that this kind of pulpit talk was
such an obvious rarity. Saddened . . . but also resolved. Resolved to
push the conversation much, much further.

I don't tell you that story to try and make myself look good,
only as one example of how the church can get more honest about
the reality of mental illness. We need to talk about it in public forms
of worship. People come to church looking and hoping to hear the
truth. It's our job as Christians to give it to them, no matter how
uncomfortable the topic may be. After all, we have somehow managed to talk an awful lot about sex, money, and politics in church. I
think it's time we made room for mental illness too.

MENTAL ILLNESS

A Most Brief History

Part of the reason mental illness is so widely misunderstood is because most of us don't have any historical context in which to frame it. The following history is embarrassingly brief but hopefully helpful for understanding just how long mental illness has been around and how difficult a problem it has posed.

IT'S JUST THE DEVIL TALKING

In 2005, a nun by the name of Maricica Irina Cornici was bound to a cross, gagged with a towel, and denied food and water for three days, after which she died. In the days prior to her death she had been hearing voices, which she attributed to the Devil, telling her she was a sinful woman. A monk named Daniel Petru Corogeanu, along with some nuns, killed her in an effort to exorcise the "demons" causing her this distress. For these heinous acts they were excommunicated from the Romanian Orthodox Church and tried and convicted in a court of law. Nevertheless, at the trial, the monk continued to believe he had done the right thing, telling a reporter, "You can't drive the devil out of people with pills. God has performed a miracle for her; finally, Irina is delivered from evil."[1]

The pills Father Daniel referenced were the medication Irina had been taking for schizophrenia, which a psychiatrist had diagnosed her with before she entered the convent. The monk and the nuns were aware of her diagnosis. Cornici was suffering from delusional thinking and auditory hallucinations, both of which are symptoms of schizophrenia. But rather than allow her to return to her doctor for treatment, they crucified her instead.

Though this happened in the recent past, the theme of blaming the Devil is not a new one. Because the progression of understanding what causes mental illness has not been linear but circular, and because what is considered abnormal differs from culture to culture and age to age, certain theories and themes about how mental illness should be treated have appeared, disappeared, and then reappeared over the centuries.

In the ancient world it was common to think of the mentally ill as demon possessed. How else to explain someone who rambles incoherently, hears voices from unseen people, or is determined to leap off the edge of a rocky cliff? In Europe, during the Middle Ages, the Roman Catholic Church prescribed prayer, confession, and exorcism as the primary means of treatment. If a woman was suffering from signs of mental illness and thus thought to have made a pact with the Devil, she was deemed a witch and burned at the stake. Some scholars estimate nearly one hundred thousand women died in this horrific manner.[2]

One form of treatment for extreme cases of mental illness throughout the ancient world was trephining: A small hole was made in a person's skull to release spirits from the body. Most people treated in this manner died, but some recovered skulls have shown signs of healing, meaning the "patient" survived the operation long enough for the body to begin repairing itself. This practice kept up for centuries, likely because it *did* blunt unwanted behavior, not by exorcising demons but by inflicting permanent brain damage.

Fortunately, the numbers of people who believe mental illness is caused by the Devil or spirits have dwindled over the centuries, but Cornici's story shows how dangerous these misinformed views have been and can continue to be for the mentally ill.

It is true that as Christians our faith asks that we believe in spirits unseen—both holy and unholy. The gospel of Mark, for example, is widely considered to be the oldest and most historically accurate account of Jesus' life. And it's Mark's gospel that goes to great lengths to describe Jesus' work as an exorcist. That being the case, I am not denying the reality of demon possession or that it might, at times, play a role in mental illness. What I am saying is that assuming mental illness is caused by demons is an outdated and potentially very dangerous position to take, as evidenced by deaths like Cornici's, may she rest in peace.

DISTURBED PHYSIOLOGY

Dissatisfied with supernatural explanations of mental illness, ancient Greek physicians went looking elsewhere for the cause. Around 400 BCE Hippocrates took a nice crack at the problem by arguing the cause of mental illness lay not with the Devil but in the balance of bodily fluids.

His theory was that people had four basic temperaments: sanguine (optimistic), choleric (irritable), melancholic (pensive), and phlegmatic (peaceful). Governing these four temperaments were four humors (bodily fluids): blood, yellow bile, black bile, and phlegm. Whatever mix of humors a person had determined the personality displayed. That meant that a depressed person simply had too much black bile. Time to get rid of it! A person who was too temperamental had too much blood and was treated with bloodletting. Fun!

While obviously wrong about the fluids, Hippocrates was right to identify the root cause of illness as originating in a person's body as opposed to forces outside of the body trying to invade. Moreover, Hippocrates did not believe mental illness was something to be ashamed of, nor did he blame patients for their unwanted behavior. For those reasons alone, he deserves a lot of credit for pushing history in the right direction.

SEGREGATION FROM SOCIETY

Another way we've historically treated people with mental illness is by keeping them separate. Throughout the Middles Ages and well into the seventeenth century it was not uncommon for the mentally ill to be segregated completely from society, either chained to dungeon walls with dangerous criminals or forced to live in isolated communities, much like lepers in the ancient world. A person who was lucky enough to not be viewed as dangerous might have been simply ignored and left to wander the streets.

The eighteenth century brought with it the first asylums, institutions designed and created for the expressed purpose of housing the mentally ill. Asylums were a step in the right direction, but they were not intended to actually treat mental illness but ostracize those who suffered from it. While certainly preferable to a dank dungeon, many of the asylums retained the draconian practice of keeping people in windowless rooms and chained to beds. Hardly any attention was given to providing people with access to caregivers.

By the end of the eighteenth century, rumblings about the inhumane conditions of these asylums began to rise up, and protests shortly followed. In 1785 Italian physician Vincenzo Chiarugi (1759–1820) removed his patients' chains at St. Boniface hospital in Florence, Italy, and began counseling his patients to take care of their hygiene. Most famously, Philippe Pinel (1745–1826) also removed the chains from his patients in France, taking them out of the dark and into the light, both literally and metaphorically. He allowed them to live in rooms with windows and took time to listen and talk with them. Pinel went so far as to encourage his patients to move freely about the asylum grounds and explore purposeful activities.

Like Hippocrates before him, Pinel did a great service to the mentally ill by seeing them as more than their illness. Speaking of those for whom he cared, Pinel said, "I cannot but give enthusiastic witness to their moral qualities. Never, except in romances, have I seen spouses more worthy to be cherished, more tender fathers, passionate lovers, purer or more magnanimous patriots, than I have seen in hospitals for the insane."[3]

TREATING AND NOT JUST HOUSING

Speaking of hospitals, the first with the expressed mission of actually treating and not just housing the mentally ill supplanted the asylum system. Building on Pinel's beliefs that the mentally ill could recover if treated with kindness, mental hospitals eschewed the arcane practices of the asylums in favor of more humane treatment. Patients were now given access to serene settings and the opportunity to engage in meaningful work and play.

The first such institution in the United States that sought to fully implement Pinel's approach was the Friends Asylum (confusing name, I know) established by the Quakers of Philadelphia in 1814. A plethora of private hospitals followed suit, each one working hard to offer patients quiet and secluded settings that held the promise of recovery.

Seeing the success of these private hospitals, a schoolteacher named Dorothea Dix began arguing that every mentally ill person in America—not just those who could afford a private hospital—ought to receive the kind of humane care being offered. Dix was extraordinarily persuasive, and by the 1870s nearly every state had a publicly funded hospital for the mentally ill.[4]

DEINSTITUTIONALIZATION

Institutionalization, as the state-funded system was known, lasted for less than a hundred years. Even though the institutions vastly improved patient care, like many governmental efforts, they were understaffed, underbudgeted, and overcrowded. It wasn't long before conditions in these hospitals began to resemble the asylums they had replaced. Handcuffing patients to their beds, even putting some in cages, became commonplace practices. As the public became aware of just how bad it had gotten at the turn of the twentieth century, there was once again pressure to reform the system.

This time, however, the solution wasn't to establish a new

kind of hospital but to release patients *from* the hospitals. Deinstitutionalization, as it came to be known in the 1960s, was done with the best of intentions. The idea was to give patients who seemed well enough to recover the opportunity to go out into the world and do just that. The hope was that, through a combination of mental health communities, antipsychotic drugs, electroconvulsive therapy, and the advent of Sigmund Freud's psychoanalysis—also known as the "talking cure"—the mentally ill would find all they needed to live happy and productive lives.

The results of deinstitutionalization remain a mixed bag. Hoping to integrate the severely mentally ill back into society represented another leap forward in progress. Unfortunately, the country wasn't prepared for the number of patients who left the hospitals, and many of them fell through the cracks. The mental health community centers that were promised never realized their full potential, and many patients found themselves living on the streets or worse.

Today our prisons are the largest mental health-care providers in the country—a fate that feels tragically circular. I would have hoped that by the twenty-first century we would be beyond the dungeons of the Middle Ages. But, alas, here we are.

A PRIMER ON DEPRESSION
AND ANXIETY

Anxiety disorders are the most common mental illnesses in America, affecting forty million adults ages eighteen and older.[1] At its most basic level, anxiety is when you feel fearful without any danger being present. It is the sense that something is about to go very wrong without any evidence suggesting this is actually the case. Those of us who battle anxiety, or have a panic disorder like me, envision the plane crashing, coronavirus spreading to everyone they know, and the house foreclosing. We catastrophize situations, jumping to almost any and every worst-case scenario. We don't want to be this way, but we are this way.

In between spells of anxiety come waves of despair. When I was suffering more deeply from my anxiety, without warning I would be overwhelmed by feelings of hopelessness and worthlessness. I felt as though the world was too cruel to live in and that I had nothing of value to add to make it any better. I didn't really have language for any of these feelings, so I kept most of them deep inside me. At a certain point I accepted this was my lot in life. Like many Christians, I believed that this was "my cross to bear." What I needed to do was suck it up and manage it. Which is what I did for a very, very long time. I lived with untreated depression and anxiety.

It's not unusual for a person with an anxiety disorder to also battle depression. In fact, nearly half of those diagnosed with depression also receive an anxiety disorder diagnosis,[2] increasingly leading mental health professionals to see these disorders as two sides to the same coin. While not synonymous, it is becoming increasingly difficult to have a meaningful discussion about anxiety without also talking about depression, and vice versa.

A few words need to be said about what I mean when I use the words *depression* and *anxiety* because every person gets sad or nervous from time to time. That's not what I'm talking about. The kind of depression and anxiety I'm describing is the kind that rises to the level of warranting clinical attention. Remember, the National Alliance on Mental Illness (NAMI) defines mental illnesses as "medical conditions that disrupt a person's thinking, feeling, mood, ability to relate to others" and "often result in a diminished capacity for coping with the ordinary demands of life."[3] *That* is the kind of depression and anxiety I'm talking about, the kind that thwarts the abundant living we hope to have—the kind that hampers our journey back to God.

Because trust me, when taking a shower feels like a monumental task, you ain't making it to Bible study. And if you're too frozen in fear to back the car out of the garage, that mission trip–planning meeting you had scheduled is getting postponed. Depression and anxiety are not conditions you can simply power through. We're not talking about a sprained ankle or the common cold. Mental illness must be tended to with great care and given the respect it deserves. Sometimes the work of the day, even if it's work done for Jesus, cannot get done because of depression and anxiety.

Depression is a force so powerful that it makes sadness seem like child's play. We all have bad days. No one feels great all of the time. But, unlike illnesses that only target a specific area of the body, the mood disorder called depression is a tsunami that washes over every square inch of an individual, both seen and unseen, affecting the entirety of that person's existence.

Depression is caused primarily by biological, environmental, and psychological factors. That means, like all forms of mental illness, it is *not* caused by sin, character defects, or a lack of Christian faith. It is a medical condition every bit as real as diabetes and cancer. Like those illnesses, it almost always requires formal treatment for long-term recovery.

Depression can afflict a person at any age, but it often begins during the teenage years or early adulthood. It can co-occur with other illnesses like cancer or heart disease, sometimes making these conditions more severe and vice versa. Depression can also be brought on by certain medications and their side effects.

After puberty, women become approximately twice as likely as men to experience depression.[4] As with all causes of mental illness, there is debate about why this is, but the hormonal argument appears fairly persuasive. Estrogen, which women produce more of than men, appears to encourage rumination, which is often a forerunner to depression. Conversely, men produce much higher degrees of testosterone, which some researchers believe actually prohibits, to a degree, self-reflective thinking.

While hormones appear to play a role in the discrepancy between the genders, some researchers posit it could also be related to the unique challenges of pregnancy and raising children. Regardless of the gender discrepancy for depression, treatment for the disorder is the same. Both men and women respond comparably to evidence-based forms of treatment when pregnancy is not a complicating factor.

ARE YOU DEPRESSED?

It's impossible to provide a comprehensive list for how depression manifests in each person because the disease is mysterious and no two people seem to suffer its ill effects in precisely the same manner. What those who suffer do hold in common is an anguish that is universally described as being indescribable. This might be one of the reasons depression so often goes undiagnosed. Some research suggests that up to two out of every five people with depression do not get the treatment they need because their symptoms are either not identified or misdiagnosed.

As you can see, diagnosing depression is far from a simple task. In an effort to take this indescribable illness and transform it into something more tangible, clinicians seek to observe a certain set of symptoms, then use those as a diagnostic tool. It's not a perfect methodology, but, for the moment, it's the best we have.

Assuming a mental health professional accepts insurance, a depression diagnosis must be made using the symptom checklist provided in the *DSM-5*. To meet the *DSM-5* criteria for diagnosis, a person needs to be experiencing five or more symptoms that represent a change from previous functioning during the same two-week period. At least one of the symptoms must be either (1) depressed mood or (2) loss of interest or pleasure.

To receive a diagnosis of depression, these symptoms must cause the individual clinically significant distress or impairment in social, occupational, or other important areas of functioning. The symptoms must also not be a result of substance abuse or another medical condition.

DSM-5 DIAGNOSTIC CRITERIA

1. "Depressed most of the day, nearly every day as indicated by either subjective report (e.g., feels sad, empty, or hopeless) or observation made by others (e.g., appears tearful)."

Everyone experiences sadness. Life is nothing if not a series of ups and downs. The kind of low mood needed to check off this symptom is one that feels like it's becoming dominant in the individual's life. Instead of feeling sad due to a life event (something known as reactive sadness), the person simply feels a general sadness or hopelessness about life without being able to articulate exactly why. It is as if a cloud of emptiness has descended that refuses to lift. Note that the *DSM* says this symptom can be met even if the patient does not report feeling sad but is observed to be sad by others. Many depressed people, for a plethora of reasons, will deny feeling depressed most of the time, thus making the observations of people who know them highly valuable.

2. "Markedly diminished interest or pleasure in all, or almost all, activities most of the day, nearly every day (as indicated by subjective account or observation)."

This is one of the more common symptoms of depression. The clinical term is *anhedonia*, and it describes a patient's loss of interest in activities they have historically enjoyed. The lack of interest, however, is not just confined to particular hobbies. Many patients will describe not being able to enjoy anything in life. A glass of water no longer feels refreshing. Sex does not entice or satisfy. The warmth of the sun is ignored. Some patients describe feeling as though life has lost its color or music, its rhythm. This is usually one of the more frightening symptoms of depression because a patient can intellectually understand that certain aspects of life should bring joy. The dissonance between knowing this and yet not feeling that joy can be quite jarring.

3. "Significant weight loss when not dieting or weight gain or decrease or increase in appetite nearly every day."

For many depressed people, eating becomes incredibly difficult. The mere thought of eating can induce nausea or other physical reactions. In a more typical case, the patient will continue to eat, albeit fewer calories than when not depressed, but report that this is only because food is critical for survival. The experience of tasting the food provides no enjoyment whatsoever.

4. "Insomnia or hypersomnia nearly every day."

Sleep is almost always disrupted by depression because the illness affects a person's circadian rhythm, the biological cycle of sleeping and waking. Falling or remaining asleep becomes difficult. Others report sleeping "all the time." One of the more common reports of depressed patients is they wake up far earlier than they want to (usually predawn) and are then unable to fall back asleep despite feeling exhausted.

5. "Psychomotor agitation or retardation nearly every day (observable by others; not merely subjective feelings of restlessness or being slowed down)."

All of us move our bodies in ways we don't actively think about. We cross our legs. Then we uncross them. We fidget around in our seats while listening to a sermon. A depressed person sometimes experiences a change in these psychomotor movements. Most often this manifests as a slowing down in these movements or a blunting of them almost altogether. Think of a person who appears either highly restless or looks sedated. The change can move in either direction. Note that, as is the case with sadness, this symptom can be met by the report of others and not just subjective reporting, as the patient might not be aware these changes are occurring.

6. "Fatigue or loss of energy nearly every day."

A depressed person often reports feeling tired regardless of the amount of rest. Routine tasks such as making the bed in the morning or getting dressed for the day feel as though they require the energy of an Olympic marathoner. What was once accomplished without so much as a single thought to the effort involved can now feel like an impossibility. When a person feels this way, exercise can become unthinkable. From the outside, others might perceive the person to be lazy because they cannot appreciate just how difficult it is to move about an ordinary day while in this condition. It is not unusual for a patient experiencing this symptom to worry that a physical illness might be causing the lack of energy. It is also not uncommon for this symptom to prompt others to urge the patient to simply snap out of it.

7. "Feelings of worthlessness or excessive or inappropriate guilt . . . nearly every day."

From time to time every person behaves in ways they regret and subsequently feel guilty about. This is not only normal but also a healthy sign that your moral compass is properly aligned. Excessive guilt, however, is not healthy and often a sign of depression. For the depressed person, pervasive guilt can sometimes cloud the mind in such a way that it overshadows any other feeling, leaving only the sensation of worthlessness.

8. "Diminished ability to think or concentrate, or indecisiveness, nearly every day."

A lot of people conceive of depression as a purely emotional issue, but for many who suffer the affliction the most noticeable symptoms are cognitive. Yes, the patient feels sad, but the more frustrating aspect is the inability to concentrate on anything, even pleasure pastimes like television shows or novels. No matter what is placed before the person's attention, the mind tends to wander aimlessly, making it hard for the patient to accomplish a given task or even recall what has been done. Many patients report that standard conversations with friends and family become difficult to follow because their minds cannot seem to stay in one place. This can become especially frustrating for the patient who is looking to find a momentary distraction from suffering by taking pleasure in simple joys like playing with a child or watching a good movie. Not even these sorts of activities provide relief.

9. "Recurrent thoughts of death . . . recurrent suicidal ideation without a specific plan, or a suicide attempt or a specific plan for committing suicide."

It is common for a person experiencing depression to consider death. When depression becomes truly severe, death is often seen as the only way to find relief. Recurrent suicidal ideation without a specific plan means the patient repeatedly thinks about dying without actively making a plan to do so. Suicidal ideation with a specific plan is a more serious situation. A past suicide attempt puts the patient at even greater risk for another.[5]

THINKING PATTERNS THAT ARE SYMPTOMATIC OF DEPRESSION AND ANXIETY

Some other symptoms of depression and anxiety manifest through specific thinking patterns that, while unhealthy and inaccurate, nonetheless persist. Here's a quick rundown of what some of those patterns are:

All-or-Nothing Thinking

Commonly referred to as black-and-white thinking, this kind of thinking refuses to recognize life as running along a continuum with never-ending shades of gray. Instead, things are either all good or all bad. You operate in absolutes, seeing each failure as a total disaster. *I failed the exam! I'll be a failure my whole life!*

Disproportionate Weight

Minor events take on epic proportions, making any duty or task feel as though you are being weighed down by the whole world. *I cannot believe she asked me to run that errand when I already have to go to work today and will be exhausted by the time I get home. I should probably call in sick to work, otherwise I simply won't be able to accomplish what I need to today. I'm so stressed out.*

Overgeneralization

Believing that any negative situation is simply further proof that you are stuck in a cycle where only bad things happen again and again. People who are stuck in this way of thinking tend to use words like *always* and *never* a lot. *Of course I am the only one whose flight was delayed. This kind of thing always happens to me. I am going to miss all the fun. I knew I should have booked my flight when my friends did. I will never fly this airline again. Why am I always so dumb about these sorts of things?*

Mental Filter

Refusing to see the good in any situation in order to focus wholly on the negative. *I wasn't expecting the raise I received at work today. I'm gonna have to make sure I save so much more money to pay for all the taxes that will be due at the end of the year. I can't believe I didn't see this coming. How could I be so naive?*

Grandiose Self-Image

People who are depressed are often described by friends as acting selfish. This is because a bout with depression or anxiety is truly a self-focused experience. It's one of the more difficult aspects of the disorder. Patients often talk of desperately wanting to get out of their own heads, but in their own heads is where they continually find themselves because they cannot find any other place to go. *I wonder how I'm gonna feel when I wake up tomorrow? Today was absolutely miserable. If I feel even half this bad, there's no way I can go to school or meet Dan for that coffee. I need to go to sleep if I'm going to get up early enough to go for a run, which will hopefully make me feel better. I can never fall asleep when I want to. I just know I'm gonna feel terrible in the morning and nothing is going to go right. I should probably call Dan right now and cancel. Or maybe I should wait until the morning? But I don't wanna do it at the last second. He'll be upset with me. I don't know what to do. I just wanna fall asleep. Should I text Dan?*

Fortune Telling

This distortion convinces you that you can predict the future, and the future will only be bad. Tomorrow will be just as bad as today if not worse. Nothing is ever going to change. *I hate my job. Every day it's the same old thing. I should probably just quit.*

Labeling (also called Name Calling)

Thinking and saying purely negative things about yourself or others. This is the toxic inner monologue. *Why was I so stupid in that meeting yesterday? I knew what my boss was going to ask me, and I knew what he wanted me to say. So why didn't I just say it? What is wrong with me? Seriously, I never get anything right. Not even the easy stuff. And why did my boss have to ask me that question anyway? He picks on me constantly. He knew I knew the answer. He should have asked someone else. He never asks anyone else. It's because he hates me. I know he hates me. Which is fine because I hate him too.*

Should Statements

Constantly telling yourself that you should do this or you must do that. *I have to get out of bed earlier tomorrow. If I don't get out of bed when my alarm clock goes off, I am such a loser.*

Mind Reading

Believing you can know what other people are thinking without any real evidence to inform you of your opinion. *Whenever I arrive at a party, people are always talking about the fact that my girlfriend and I broke up. It doesn't matter that it's been six months. It happens every time I walk in. People stop talking and glance over at me before trying to muffle their laughter. Why are they so obsessed with my life? I can't take this anymore. I wish they would just mind their own business and leave me alone.*

Blaming

Believing that your behavior is the cause of other people's actions. This could be positive or negative. The point is that you believe everything going on around you is somehow a reaction to you. *If I weren't such a bore, my wife would be so much happier. She is always talking to her friends on the phone because I have nothing to say. If I were more interesting, she also wouldn't have to have that gym membership. I know she says she loves working out, but she's only doing it to get away from having to spend time with me in the evenings.*

Catastrophizing

This thought pattern takes a small matter and immediately supersizes it to something catastrophic. *I can't believe they down-sized my Christmas bonus this year. I have worked at this company for fifteen years. I know the economy is in a recession and that I managed to save a lot of money last year while getting our family completely out of debt. But this is a disaster. Downsizing my bonus must mean they are preparing to fire me. If they do, I'll never find another job. We'll be homeless soon.*

Over- or Under-spiritualizing

It's not uncommon for depressed and anxious people to become either extremely religious or reject the religious life altogether. Neither extreme is really thought to be more helpful than the other. If a person who has always believed in God suddenly drops the belief, this could complicate feelings of depression because it will be a loss that needs mourning. Conversely, people who overspiritualize the illness of depression and place all the blame on the Devil will be less likely to examine their actual physical condition and the decisions they may or may not be making. *If I would just pray harder, I know my depression would lift. The Devil is so intent on keeping me unhappy that he is interfering with my faith. I just have to go to church every Sunday and tithe even more money. If I show the Devil how faithful I am, he will eventually give up and leave me alone.*

Loss of Control

Anxious people are particularly prone to this thought pattern, especially if they have suffered from panic attacks. They begin to fear they will lose total control over themselves and then subsequently every other aspect of their lives. *If I can't control my own nerves, how am I ever going to get anything done? I can't even drive down the street without having a panic attack. Nothing will ever be the same now. I've completely lost the ability to control my own mind, which means I have absolutely no chance at living the life I actually want. I am doomed. I can't believe this is happening to me.*

If you identify with the above thought patterns and any of the nine diagnostic observations in the previous section, I urge you to reach out to a professional for help. Please know that depression and anxiety do not usually go away on their own but almost always require clinical treatment. These are serious disorders that can rob joy from life and sometimes even life itself. But there are so many ways to find healing. Please, I beg of you, avail yourself of them.

COMMON SIGNS OF SUICIDAL THOUGHTS AND BEHAVIORS

1. TALKING ABOUT ENDING THEIR LIFE

Many suicidal people will express a desire to die in their language. They may not explicitly state they want to kill themselves but might say things like:

- "I don't think anyone would really miss me if I were gone."
- "I don't think I'll be around much longer."
- "I want all of this to just end."
- "I am so tired of how my life never changes."

2. GUILT

Many suicidal people will express excessive amounts of guilt, convinced that they are truly terrible with no hope of redemption. Their language is often fraught with self-loathing phrases like:

- "I wish I had never been born."
- "Nobody really loves me anyway."
- "Why should anyone love me when I don't love myself?"

3. FEELING HELPLESS OR HOPELESS

When a person can no longer find solutions to life's problems, suicide can become a more attractive option. Feeling as though there will be no resolution to pain or a troubling circumstance can put a person at risk of suicide. A person who feels this way may say things like:

- "It doesn't matter what I try. Nothing works."
- "Why should I keep trying when nothing ever changes?"
- "I can't. I just can't anymore. I'm done."
- "What difference does it make?"

4. WITHDRAWING FROM FRIENDS AND FAMILY

Depressed people commonly withdraw from intimate relationships. If a person is suicidal, this withdrawal is likely to be even more extreme. The person may stop replying to messages from friends, cancel plans at the last minute, or spend inordinate amounts of time staying home or even in bed, not doing much of anything except sleeping. Some suggest this withdrawal is the person's unconscious attempt to prepare for death.

5. GIVING AWAY TREASURED POSSESSIONS

Suicidal people often give away the things they love most. They'll often ask friends to promise to care for their children or pets if anything were to ever happen to them. A depressed person who suddenly becomes highly interested in settling financial affairs or preparing a will should be watched closely.

6. INCREASED USE OF ALCOHOL OR OTHER DRUGS

It's not uncommon for depressed people to increase the amount of alcohol they're consuming in an attempt to cope with their pain. Any time there is a dramatic increase in use of any substance, we need to pay close attention, but especially with someone we fear is suicidal. Sometimes suicidal people will mix prescription drugs and alcohol to tempt fate. This kind of behavior needs to be taken seriously because it could indicate the individual is seriously suicidal.

7. PREOCCUPATION WITH PEOPLE WHO HAVE DIED BY SUICIDE

Because suicide is so scary, it's only natural that many of us find it interesting. That said, a suicidal person who begins spending large amounts of time following news stories or reading about other people who have died by suicide could be indicating an intent to act.

8. A PLAN

If a person has taken the time to draw up a plan for suicide, this should be seen as one of the most serious warning signs. Any person with a suicide plan needs immediate psychiatric attention.

9. PREVIOUS SUICIDE ATTEMPTS

Any history of self-harm or suicide attempts puts a person at great risk for suicide. If you know someone who has attempted in the past and has begun self-harming, this is a serious warning sign.

If you ever feel this way yourself, please know you have several options for getting immediate assistance:

1. Dial 911. Tell the operator you're suicidal, and then stay on the line and do exactly as you are told. Help will be on the way before you know it.
2. Call the National Suicide Prevention Lifeline at 1-800-273-TALK (8255). A trained volunteer will answer your call.
3. Text START to 741-741. An actual human being who is trained to help you with your situation will immediately text you back. Pretty cool, huh?
4. If you're young and a member of the LGBTQ+ community, you may consider reaching out to The Trevor Project, which provides free, confidential support 24-7 to LGBTQ youth via a helpline, text, and online instant messaging system. Call 1-866-488-7386 for their services.
5. If you're a veteran, you may feel comfortable contacting the Veterans Crisis Line, which provides free, confidential support 24-7 to veterans, active service members, and their family and friends in times of need. Call 1-800-273-8255 and press 1 or text 838-255 for support.

SUGGESTED READING

FOR THE PERSON BATTLING ANXIETY:

Reasons to Stay Alive by Matt Haig

FOR THE PERSON BATTLING DEPRESSION:

Darkness Visible: A Memoir of Madness by William Styron

FOR THE PERSON LOVING SOMEONE WITH MENTAL ILLNESS:

When Someone You Love Is Depressed: How to Help Your Loved One Without Losing Yourself by Laura Epstein Rosen and Xavier Francisco Amador

FOR THE PASTOR BATTLING SERIOUS MENTAL ILLNESS:

Darkness Is My Only Companion: A Christian Response to Mental Illness by Kathryn Greene-McCreight

FOR THE PERSON INTERESTED IN READING AN ENGROSSING, TRUE-LIFE NARRATIVE ABOUT THE INS AND OUTS OF PSYCHOTHERAPY:

Maybe You Should Talk to Someone: A Therapist, Her *Therapist, and Our Lives Revealed* by Lori Gottlieb

FOR THE PERSON CONCERNED ABOUT THEIR DRINKING AND WANTING A
SCIENTIFIC APPROACH TO ALCOHOL:

*This Naked Mind: Control Alcohol, Find Freedom, Discover
Happiness & Change Your Life* by Annie Grace

ACKNOWLEDGMENTS

I'd like to first thank my extraordinarily talented literary agent, Amanda Luedeke, for taking a chance on me. Without her belief in me and the importance of this message, this book would have never happened. I can't thank her enough for this opportunity.

I'd also like to thank Jessica Wong for saying yes to this book. Working with Jessica has been nothing less than a dream come true. Jessica made this book exponentially better than I ever imagined it could be. I spent years wondering what it would be like to work with someone of her caliber. The experience did not disappoint. The same goes for Brigitta Nortker, who also edited this book. Her encouragement and helpful comments lifted my spirit when I most needed it.

Thanks to my clients who grant me the honor of joining their interior lives on a daily basis. I count this a sacred privilege.

I offer a heart full of love and appreciation to my wife, Caroline, for standing by me through all of my own struggles and allowing me the space and time to do this insane thing we call writing. I can do nothing without you. I wouldn't even want to try. You have my heart.

Finally, Mom and Dad, thank you for never giving up on me. You showed me the Good Way as a child, and you helped me back to the road when I got lost in the woods. I love you, I love you, I love you.

NOTES

Introduction

1. The Episcopal Church, *The Book of Common Prayer* (New York: Church Publishing, 2007), 327.

Chapter 1: You're Not Alone

1. Jamie Tworkowski, *If You Feel Too Much* (New York: Jeremy P. Tarcher/Penguin, 2015), 36.
2. Susan Johnson, *Hold Me Tight: Seven Conversations for a Lifetime of Love* (New York: Little, Brown Spark, 2008), 16.
3. Michael Dimock, "Defining Generations: Where Millennials End and Generation Z Begins," Pew Research Center, January 17, 2019, https://www.pewresearch.org/fact-tank/2019/01/17/where-millennials-end-and-generation-z-begins/.
4. Cigna, *Cigna U.S. Loneliness Index*, May 2018, https://www.multivu.com/players/English/8294451-cigna-us-loneliness-survey/docs/IndexReport_1524069371598-173525450.pdf.

Mental Health: True or False?

1. National Institute of Mental Health Disorders, "Statistics Related to Mental Health Disorders," John Hopkins Medicine, https://www.hopkinsmedicine.org/health/wellness-and-prevention/mental-health-disorder-statistics; Bruce Japsen, "Psychiatrist

Shortage Escalates as U.S. Mental Health Needs Grow," *Forbes*, February 25, 2018, https://www.forbes.com/sites/brucejapsen /2018/02/25/psychiatrist-shortage-escalates-as-u-s-mental-health -needs-grow/#57a2cc051255; Maggie Fox, "Veterans More Likely Than Civilians to Die by Suicide, VA Study Finds," NBC News, June 18, 2018, https://www.nbcnews.com/health/health-news /veterans-more-likely-civilians-die-suicide-va-study-finds -n884471; Centers for Disease Control and Prevention WISQARS Leading Causes of Death Reports, "Suicide," National Institute of Mental Health, last updated April 2019, https://www.nimh.nih .gov/health/statistics/suicide.shtml; https://www.ncbi.nlm.nih .gov/pmc/articles/PMC5007565/; Holly Hedegaard, Arialdi Miniño, and Margaret Warner, *Drug Overdose Deaths in the United States, 1999–2017*, NCHS Data Brief, no. 329 (Hyattsville, MD: National Center for Health Statistics, 2018), https://www.cdc .gov/nchs/data/databriefs/db329-h.pdf; Sara G. Miller, "1 in 6 Americans Takes a Psychiatric Drug," *Scientific American*, December 13, 2016, https://www.scientificamerican.com/article /1-in-6-americans-takes-a-psychiatric-drug/; LifeWay Research, *Study of Acute Mental Illness and Christian Faith*, September 2014, http://lifewayresearch.com/wp-content/uploads/2014/09/Acute -Mental-Illness-and-Christian-Faith-Research-Report-1.pdf; Donald S. Shepard et al., "Suicide and Suicidal Attempts in the United States: Costs and Policy Implications," *Suicide and Life- Threatening Behavior* 46, no. 3 (2016), https://www.sprc.org/sites /default/files/migrate/library/Shepard_SuicideAndAttemptsUS _CostsPolicyImplications2015.pdf; Helene Schumacher, "Why More Men Than Women Die by Suicide," BBC Future, March 17, 2019, https://www.bbc.com/future/article/20190313-why-more -men-kill-themselves-than-women; Rubina Kapil, "5 Surprising Mental Health Statistics," Mental Health First Aid USA, February 6, 2019, https://www.mentalhealthfirstaid.org/2019/02/5 -surprising-mental-health-statistics/.

Chapter 2: What Is Mental Health?

1. "Change Your Mind About Mental Health," American Psychological Association, 2000, https://www.apa.org/helpcenter/change.

2. Jamie Ballard, "Millennials Are the Loneliest Generation," YouGov, July 30, 2019, https://today.yougov.com/topics/lifestyle/articles -reports/2019/07/30/loneliness-friendship-new-friends-poll-survey.

3. Chris Jackson and Negar Ballard, "Over Half of Americans Report Feeling Like No One Knows Them Well," Ipsos, May 1, 2018, https://www.ipsos.com/en-us/news-polls/us-loneliness-index-report.

4. John T. Cacioppo and Stephanie Cacioppo, "The Growing Problem of Loneliness," *Lancet* 391, no. 10119 (February 2018): 426, https://doi .org/10.1016/S0140–6736(18)30142-9.

5. Julianne Holt-Lunstad et al., "Loneliness and Social Isolation as Risk Factors for Mortality: A Meta-Analytic Review," *Perspectives on Psychological Science* 10, no. 2 (March 2015), https://doi.org /10.1177/1745691614568352.

6. "Mental Health: Strengthening Our Response," World Health Organization, March 30, 2018, https://www.who.int/news-room /fact-sheets/detail/mental-health-strengthening-our-response.

Chapter 3: What Is Mental Illness?

1. Randolph M. Neese, *Good Reasons for Bad Feelings* (New York: Dutton, 2019), 9.

2. American Psychiatric Association, *Diagnostic and Statistical Manual of Mental Disorders*, 5th ed. (Washington, DC: American Psychiatric Association, 2013), 20.

3. Neese, *Good Reasons for Bad Feelings*, 8.

4. According to the National Alliance on Mental Health (NAMI) at least four hundred thousand currently incarcerated individuals in the United States suffer from mental illness. NAMI also estimates that between 25 and 40 percent of all mentally ill Americans "will be jailed or incarcerated at some point in their lives." Matt Ford, "America's Largest Mental Hospital Is a Jail," *Atlantic*, June 8, 2015,

https://www.theatlantic.com/politics/archive/2015/06/americas
-largest-mental-hospital-is-a-jail/395012/.

5. Jordan W. Smoller, "Psychiatric Genetics Begins to Find Its
   Footing," *American Journal of Psychiatry* 176, no. 8 (August 2019),
   https://doi.org/10.1176/appi.ajp.2019.19060643.
6. Timothy J. Legg, "Is Depression Genetic?" Healthline, July 25, 2017,
   https://www.healthline.com/health/depression/genetic.
7. Steven D. Hollon and Philip K. Kendall, "Cognitive Self-Statements in
   Depression: Development of an Automatic Thoughts Questionnaire,"
   Cognitive Therapy and Research 4, no. 4 (1980): 388–89, https://doi
   .org/10.1007/BF01178214.
8. Derald Wing Sue and David Sue, *Counseling the Culturally Diverse:
   Theory and Practice*, 3rd ed. (Hoboken, NJ: John Wiley & Sons, 1999).
9. Eli Rosenberg, "'I'm Done Hiding This': Jason Kander Pulls Out
   of Mayor's Race, Citing PTSD and Depression," *Washington Post*,
   October 2, 2018, https://www.washingtonpost.com/politics/2018
   /10/02/im-done-hiding-this-rising-star-jason-kander-pulls-out
   -mayors-race-citing-ptsd-depression/.

Chapter 4: Why Does God Allow Mental Illness?

1. John Holmes, "Losing 25,000 to Hunger Every Day," *UN Chronicle*
   45, no. 2 & 3 (April 2008), https://unchronicle.un.org/article/losing
   -25000-hunger-every-day.
2. Reeve Robert Brenner, *The Faith and Doubt of Holocaust Survivors*
   (New Brunswick, NJ: Transaction Publishers, 2014), 102.
3. Elie Wiesel, *Night* (New York: Hill and Wang, 2012).

Chapter 5: This Is Not a Drill

1. Gary Greenberg, "The Rats of N.I.M.H.," *New Yorker*, May 16, 2013,
   https://www.newyorker.com/tech/annals-of-technology/the-rats
   -of-n-i-m-h.
2. Matthew S. Stanford and Kandace R. McAlister, "Perceptions of
   Serious Mental Illness in the Local Church," *Journal of Religion,
   Disability & Health* 12, no. 2 (October 2008), https://doi.org/10.1080
   /15228960802160654.

3. Ryan Casey Waller (Christians and Mental Health), "Question: If the following vignette is something that has happened to you, and you feel comfortable talking about it, would you mind private messaging me," Facebook, October 21, 2019, https://www.facebook .com/ChristiansandMentalHealth/posts/2489930661103885.

Mental Health Myth

1. Bethany Verrett, "What Does the Bible Say About Suicide?" Bible Study Tools, December 17, 2019, https://www.biblestudytools.com /bible-study/topical-studies/bible-says-about-suicide.html.

2. Steve and Robyn Bloem, *Broken Minds: Hope for Healing When You Feel Like You're Losing It* (Grand Rapids: Kregel, 2005), 204.

Chapter 6: Abundant Life for All

1. Andrew Court and Jennifer Smith, "Pictured: Mother Who Pushed Her 16-Month-Old Son and Daughter, Four, off Parking Garage Roof Then Leaped to Her Death on Christmas Day in Double Murder-Suicide After an 'Argument with Her Husband,'" *Daily Mail*, December 26, 2019, https://www.dailymail.co.uk/news /article-7828553/Pictured-Mom-killed-children-double-murder -suicide.html.

2. "Preventing Recurrent Depression: Long-term Treatment for Major Depressive Disorder," *Primary Care Companion to the Journal of Clinical Psychiatry* 9, no. 3 (2007): 214–23.

3. Ranna Parekh, ed., "What Is Depression?" American Psychiatric Association, January 2017, https://www.psychiatry.org/patients -families/depression/what-is-depression.

4. Hannah Furness, "I Sought Counselling After 20 Years of Not Thinking About the Death of My Mother, Diana, and Two Years of Total Chaos in My Life," *Telegraph*, April 19, 2017, https://www .telegraph.co.uk/news/2017/04/16/prince-harry-sought-counselling -death-mother-led-two-years-total/.

5. Katie Mettler, "'All of This Grief': Prince Harry Opens Up About Mental Health, Mother's Death," *Washington Post*, April 17, 2017,

https://www.charlotteobserver.com/news/nation-world/world
/article144998779.html.

6. Mettler.
7. Mettler.
8. Mettler.

Chapter 7: Epidemic

1. Jarrid Wilson (@JarridWilson), Twitter, September 9, 2019, 4:01
   p.m., https://twitter.com/jarridwilson/status/1171166658829803520.
2. Jarrid Wilson (@JarridWilson), Twitter, September 9, 2019, 1:01
   p.m., https://twitter.com/jarridwilson/status/1171121544161976320.
3. Lily Low, "What Does Pastor Jarrid Wilson's Death Tell Us About
   Mental Health and Faith," Thrive Global, September 13, 2019,
   https://thriveglobal.com/stories/what-does-pastor-jarrid-wilsons
   -death-tell-us-about-mental-health-and-faith/.
4. Centers for Disease Control and Prevention, "Suicide."
5. "Mental Health: Suicide Data," World Health Organization, https
   ://www.who.int/mental_health/prevention/suicide/suicideprevent/en/.
6. Centers for Disease Control, "Drug Overdose Deaths," March 19,
   2020, https://www.cdc.gov/drugoverdose/data/statedeaths.html.
7. Ryan Casey Waller, Facebook, September 10, 2019, https://www
   .facebook.com/ryancaseywaller/posts/10107282206865895.

Chapter 8: The Problem of Suicide

1. Substance Abuse and Mental Health Services Administration,
   Results from the 2013 National Survey on Drug Use and Health:
   Mental Health Findings, NSDUH Series H-49, HHS Publication
   No. (SMA) 14–4887. Rockville, MD: Substance Abuse and Mental
   Health Services Administration, 2014.
2. Starr Bowenbank, "Billie Eilish Opens Up About Her History with
   Depression and Suicidal Thoughts," Cosmopolitan, January 24,
   2020, https://www.cosmopolitan.com/entertainment/celebs
   /a30653612/billie-eilish-commit-suicide-gayle-king-interviw/.
3. Nicole Einbinder, "'I Sleep All the Time, Because It's the Closest Thing to

Death': Simone Biles Talks About Facing Depression After Sexual Abuse," Insider, March 29, 2019, https://www.insider.com/gymnast-simone-biles -opens-up-about-facing-depression-after-sexual-abuse-2019-3.

4. Pope John Paul II, *Catechism of the Catholic Church* (Vatican City: Libereria Editrice Vaticana, 1993), 3.2.2.5, http://w2.vatican.va /archive/ccc_css/archive/catechism/p3s2c2a5.htm.

5. G. K. Chesterton, *Orthodoxy* (New York: John Lane Company, 1908), 131–32.

6. Jonathan T. O. Cavanagh et al., "Psycholgical Autopsy Studies of Suicide: A Systemic Review," *Psychological Medicine* 33, no. 3 (April 2003), https://doi.org/10.1017/S0033291702006943.

7. "Suicide Prevention," National Institute of Mental Health, last revised July 2019, https://www.nimh.nih.gov/health/topics/suicide -prevention/index.shtml.

8. Henri Nouwen, *Out of Solitude* (Notre Dame, IN: Ave Maria Press, 2004), 38.

9. Jeffrey A. Bridge et al., "Association Between the Release of Netflix's *13 Reasons Why* and Suicide Rates in the United States: An Interrupted Time Series Analysis," *Journal of the American Academy of Child & Adolescent Psychiatry* 59, no. 2 (February 2020), https://doi.org/10.1016/j.jaac.2019.04.020.

Suicide Myths

1. College of Central Florida, "Suicide Myths and Facts," https://www .cf.edu/go/assistance/special-programs/suicide-prevention/suicide -myths-facts.

2. "Teen Suicide Is Preventable," American Psychological Association, https://www.apa.org/research/action/suicide.

Chapter 9: Who Are We?

1. Richard Rohr, *Immortal Diamond: The Search for Our True Self* (San Francisco: Jossey-Bass, 2013), 10.

2. David G. Benner, *Soulful Spirituality: Becoming Fully Alive and Deeply Human* (Grand Rapids, MI: Brazos Press, 2011) 10–11.

3. Brené Brown, *The Gifts of Imperfection* (Center City, MN: Hazelden, 2010), 29.

Chapter 11: Medication

1. Warren Kinghorn, "What Is Needed, Right Now, for the Journey?" *Church Health Reader*, December 21, 2017, https://chreader.org /needed-right-now-journey/.
2. Kinghorn.
3. Kinghorn.
4. Warren Kinghorn, "Prozac and Jesus: A Christian Psychiatrist's Perspective on Mental Health Medication and Following God," Center for Christian Scholarship, September 20, 2017, https://www .christianityandscholarship.org/event/prozacandjesus/.
5. William Styron, *Darkness Visible: A Memoir of Madness* (New York: Vintage Books, 1990), 62.
6. "Landmark Study Shows GeneSight˙ Test Led to Significant Improvement in Mental Health Outcomes for Patients with Major Depressive Disorder," GeneSight, May 7, 2018, https://genesight.com /landmark-study-shows-genesight-test-led-to-significant-improvement -in-mental-health-outcomes-for-patients-with-major-depressive -disorder/.

Chapter 12: People

1. Katharine Q. Seelye, "Fraction of Americans with Drug Addiction Receive Treatment, Surgeon General Says," *New York Times*, November 17, 2016, https://www.nytimes.com/2016/11/18/us /substance-abuse-surgeon-general-report.html.
2. *Modern Love*, episode 3, "Take Me as I Am, Whoever I Am," directed by John Carney, written by John Carney and Terri Cheney, featuring Anne Hathaway, Gary Carr, and Quincy Tyler Bernstein, aired October 18, 2019, on Amazon Prime Video, https://www .amazon.com/gp/video/detail/amzn1.dv.gti.06b6d631–5aba-565d -e9cd-a103ab22429a.

Chapter 13: Putting Treatment All Together

1. Ree Hines, "Brad Pitt: 'I Removed My Drinking Privileges' After Angelina Jolie Split," *Today*, https://www.today.com/popculture/brad-pitt-i-removed-my-drinking-privileges-after-angelina-jolie-t161864.

Mental Illness: A Most Brief History

1. Matthew S. Stanford, *Grace for the Afflicted: A Clinical and Biblical Perspective on Mental Illness* (Downers Grove, IL: InterVarsity Press, 2008), 21.
2. "History of Witches," History.com, updated February 21, 2020, https://www.history.com/topics/folklore/history-of-witches.
3. C. Sushma and Meghamala S. Tavaragi, "Moral Treatment: Philippe Pinel," *International Journal of Indian Psychology* 3, no. 2 (March 2016): 166, https://ijip.in/articles/moral-treatment-philippe-pinel/.
4. Patricia D'Antonio, "History of Psychiatric Hospitals," Penn Nursing, https://www.nursing.upenn.edu/nhhc/nurses-institutions-caring/history-of-psychiatric-hospitals/.

A Primer on Depression and Anxiety

1. "Facts & Statistics," Anxiety and Depression Association of America, https://adaa.org/about-adaa/press-room/facts-statistics.
2. "Facts & Statistics."
3. "What Is Mental Illness: Mental Illness Facts," NAMI Southern Arizona, http://www.namisa.org/what-is-mental-illness—types-of-mental-disorders.html.
4. "Women and Depression," Harvard Health Publishing, May 2011, https://www.health.harvard.edu/womens-health/women-and-depression.
5. American Psychiatric Association, *Diagnostic and Statistical Manual of Mental Disorders*, 5th ed. (Washington, DC: American Psychiatric Association, 2013): 160–61.

ABOUT THE AUTHOR

Ryan Casey Waller is a licensed psychotherapist, lawyer, and pastor who has heard all the jokes about being both lawyer and priest. But if you have another one, he's always game for more laughs. He studied philosophy and religion at the University of Southern California before pursuing a law degree, a masters in theology, and a masters in counseling from Southern Methodist University. He practiced law before turning to a career in ministry, serving in both academic and ecclesial settings. He is now in private practice in Dallas.